RACING HELL – THE HIDDEN TRUTHS OF MOTORSPORT

RACING HELL

THE HIDDEN TRUTHS OF MOTORSPORT

PETER CATE

Published by: Publishing Push Ltd

ISBNs:
978-1-80541-399-8 (paperback)
978-1-80541-400-1 (eBook)
978-1-80541-401-8 (hardcover)

All photographs copyright © 2023 Peter Cate
All illustrations copyright © 2023 Peter Cate
All sketches copyright © 2023 Peter Cate
Layout and Graphic Design by Peter Cate
Cover Photo Credit: Jamey Price Photo www.jameypricephoto.com

*To all who wish to progress in our sport
and to all who wish our sport to progress.*

@PeterCateRacing

ABOUT THE AUTHOR

Peter Cate continues to be a front-runner in the international motorsport arena, having competed at a high level for more than three decades. He is especially well-known for his successful ten years' driving with the Aston Martin factory team. To date, he has achieved five Nürburgring 24 hours class victories at the infamous Green Hell alongside many of the world's best drivers, together with podium finishes in the British Touring Car Championship and many other racing categories.

Prior to embarking upon a life of racing cars, Peter achieved a first-class honours degree in automotive industrial design at Coventry University. His recent creation of the Omologato 'Green Hell 25.378' watch has drawn much attention within the motor racing community.

Peter lives in the Cotswolds with his wife Kim, daughters Beth and Amelie, and vizsla Rocco.

ACKNOWLEDGEMENTS

Thank you to my parents, who lit the fire and always inspired me to aim high.

Thank you to my wife Kim, for her unwavering belief and support, even when I couldn't see the way.

Thank you to my daughters Beth and Amelie, who remind me that nothing is impossible when dreams are involved.

Thank you to Blockley Café, for the caffeine that fuelled this journey.

And thank you to everyone who believed in me, invested in me and looked after me over all these years. You know who you are.

CONTENTS

"Miss-Hit-Miss" Ex-Mühle
Lauda-Links
Bergwerk
Spiegelkurve
Kallenhard Wehrseifen Breidscheid
Kesselchen
Metzgesfeld 2
Steilstrecke Hohe Acht
Adenauer Forst Metzgesfeld 1
Klostertal
Wippermann
Mutkurve
Carraciola-Karussell
Fuchsröhre
Eschbach
Aremberg
Eiskurve
Brünnchen
Schwedenkreuz
Pflantzgarten 2
Schwalbenschwanz Pflantzgarten 1
Kottenborn
Kleine Karussell
Stefan Bellof S
Flugplatz
Galgenkopf
Döttinger Höhe
Quiddelbacher Höhe
Sabine Schmitz Antoniusbuche
Kurve
Hocheichen
Hatzenbach Tiergarten
ADVAN Bogen
Warsteiner NGK Schikane
Kurve
Dorint Am
RTL Kurve Nürburgring
Yokohama S
Michael Valvoline Kurve
Schumacher S
Ford Kurve
Dunlop Kehre

The 'GREEN HELL' Circuit Map
NÜRBURGRING 24 HOURS Configuration

Total Lap Length: 15.86 miles (25.378km)

Corners: 84   Gradient: up to 18%

Lowest point: 320m Highest Point: 620m

THE OUT LAP

Racing Hell is a collection of motor racing truths. I've drawn upon my detailed notes from more than 30 years behind the wheel with top-level teams, to share some of the very best and worst features of our sport as I have seen them. I'll detail key aspects I wish I'd known before I started racing and notable mistakes I've made since, exposing the realities of striving to compete with the best. My route through racing has been unconventional and largely independent, allowing me an impartial and unique platform from which I can reveal unfiltered memories and honest admissions, with no hidden agenda.

Although an autobiography is most definitely not the aim of this book, I do include many racing anecdotes, especially in the early chapters, to provide credibility and context for the later content, shedding light on how I was able to build my racing capabilities and know-how from childhood to my first motor races. You'll then read about incredible things that happened to me or to people around me, the awesome cars I've raced (and the not so awesome!), the top teams, the super-talented world-class team mates, the subtleties of car set-up and the breathtaking tracks that were the scenes of so many challenging contests. These experiences that made me a more competitive and more complete driver are all worth sharing, together with the camaraderie and wicked humour of the paddock!

But when the pit garage is opened, there are also dark things that live in there which need to be dragged into the light. I'll discuss taboo topics including the psychological fears, the frustrations, the fools and fraudsters and even the outrageous skulduggery of saboteurs which can make racing hell, destabilising or even crashing a driver's career at any level.

A book of this nature cannot be complete without acknowledging the importance of sponsor partnerships, the real fuel in any competitive race car and the source of most of the unfairness in our sport. I say this with no bitterness: I have proactively developed vital relationships that have sustained my driving career far longer than most. By revealing my path, I hope talented racers can find and sustain support for the breaks they deserve.

After sponsorship issues brutally cut short my own British Touring Car Championship campaigns, I discovered a different kind of racing hell: the Green Hell reinvigorated my racing ambitions, offering everything I had initially imagined motorsport would, including much I had lost along the way. I am more proud of my twenty plus Nürburgring 24 hours races than of any other of my racing successes. The Nordschleife is one of the last authentic motor racing circuits in the world. It has not been blighted with massive tarmac run-off areas, chicanes or too many other sanitising alterations. In the final chapter, I've provided an immersive experience of a night-racing lap there, the toughest of all challenges for racing drivers: if you can race the Green Hell, you can race well anywhere!

This, then, is a handbook packed with uncensored recollections of a veteran driver (as I've apparently been labelled) who somehow managed to cross over from the oily rags and muddy fields of club racing to the spotless pit garages of professional motorsport. Controversial as many of these accounts and opinions may be, my intentions are only to raise awareness and activate improvement. I suspect many who are deeply involved in the sport do not always have sufficient perspective to appreciate the slow decline of key elements that have enabled motorsport to flourish for more than a century. The foundations that built that heritage must be preserved, not obscured by the glitz and glamour, the contrived and the commercial, the monotonous and the manipulated. Truly authentic, unadulterated motorsport. That's Racing Hell.

I've had a fantastic ride; long may you enjoy the same!

Peter Cate
November 2023

IT'S IN THE BLOOD

For as long as I can remember, I have assumed I would eventually become a racing driver, even if I didn't know how. My parents' enthusiasm for motorsport must bear much of the responsibility: this manifested itself in one of my earliest memories, playing with my Matchbox cars on a picnic rug in the sunshine at our local Oulton Park track, breathing in the glorious scent of Castrol R as the drivers hustled their thundering machines around that beautiful Cheshire circuit. Back at home, we'd watch the late-night Grand Prix broadcasts on a black-and-white TV, perched upon a black-and-white upholstered settee, no doubt a subliminal chequered flag reference.

My great-grandfather owned one of the first cars in Holland. My great-aunt hill-climbed cars in Hungary. Although I never saw him compete, my dad Henny raced his own cars in the 1950s, mainly at Oulton Park, initially in a Standard 8 with somewhere in the region of 30bhp! The long circuit configuration at Oulton Park still exists today (albeit now with the Britten's chicane before Hilltop, and the Hislop's chicane before Knickerbrook) and his mates in the pits bet him a pint he'd not be able to break three minutes in that car. After much gritting of teeth, he finally saw a foaming tankard of beer crudely chalked onto his pit board!

Dad progressed to compete in a road-going AC Ace he bought second-hand. The car allegedly had never been raced, but a picture in *Autosport* magazine of the car in an accident at Silverstone said differently, along with the racing aero-screen holes already drilled into the cowl. When challenged, the dealer was kind enough to pay for a lot of remedial work on the car at the AC factory; a great lesson in knowing your stuff when it comes to purchasing the car you intend to race. Dad sold the car for £400 in 1960, realising that racing your road car is a high-risk game after being 'leant on' by another competitor through Oulton's fearsome double-apex right Druids corner. Unbelievably, the same car was bought over 50 years later for more than £300,000! Dad went on to race a self-built Mayfield Special 1172cc, a cigar-shaped open-wheeler, in 750 Motor Club events. Seeing photos of the car, the exposed driving position makes me shudder, as do the very un-aerodynamic regulation wheel arches that would flex at speed more than a Red Bull RB7 front wing!

Over the same period, Dad competed in various road rallies, famously winning the 1958 Intervarsity rally, partly thanks to the skills of his navigator Gerry. Sometimes he would navigate, a bad choice on one occasion when his co-driver lost control in a night rally, descending Hardknott Pass in the Lake District (well worth a drive, by the way) and barrel-rolling down two sections of hairpins. Incredibly, the engine fired up and they could continue, but the marshal at the next checkpoint had a hard time recognising which car it was!

These stories and more all help to explain why, when I showed interest in motor racing at a young age, Dad was happy to take me along to watch, often at Oulton Park but also further afield. We had an old Bedford CF van he'd converted into a camper and I have a fond memory of waking up one morning in July 1978 on the way back from holiday and seeing the huge Marlboro backdrops of Silverstone grandstands: I'd been asleep when we drove in and had no idea we were there to watch Nelson Piquet, Derek Warwick, Tiff Needell and others contest one of the British F3 rounds.

On the Saturday evening, we took a track walk together. A sleeping race track has a dormant energy you have to experience first-hand to appreciate. Years later, after watching Guns N' Roses at the old Wembley stadium, I left my mates and jumped over the barrier to take a wander back-stage. Grabbing hold of Axl's iconic steering-wheel mike stand, I could feel that same suppressed energy contained within it. At Silverstone I clearly remember that buzz, sitting on the tarmac looking down towards Copse corner from the original pole position spot, thinking, "I'm going to be here on pole one day." As a 'late starter', it took me 17 more years before I was driving equipment suitable enough to achieve it! After Nelson's F3 victory the next day, I was thrilled to get his autograph at the back of the pits. It was the first time I met a 'pro' driver and it was inspirational for me to realise these heroes were flesh and blood humans, like the rest of us.

We came back to Silverstone several times in the following years. One memorable visit was my first endurance race, the 1985 Istel Tourist Trophy, dominated by the TWR Bastos Rover Vitesse V8s and the equally impressive Eggenberger Nordica Volvo 240 Turbos. However, my main recollection of that event was our unorthodox late-night entry to the circuit, the security guards leaping out of the way as our Bedford camper accelerated towards them, screaming defiance with all of its 60bhp! Never one to willingly acknowledge authority (and I must admit I share some of that characteristic), Dad clearly felt Silverstone camping should still be free, literally gate-crashing the event, even if it meant we had to hide in a dark back field for an hour until the coast was clear!

With hindsight, I see all those events were a fabulous education, walking trackside with someone who could describe the details of the action from a racer's perspective, understanding the reasons why drivers were quick or slow. At the same time, there was no golden ticket for me to enter a junior racing category, nor was there a racing kart waiting in the garage on Christmas morning. In fact, I still remember Dad's adaptation of 'Ding Dong! Merrily on High': "And I owe, I owe, I owe, the bank a lot of money!" He was a dentist with little free time or spare funds and very much of the opinion that I should concentrate on my studies. Although I couldn't see it in those days, he has since been proved right in so many ways, as later chapters will show.

Nevertheless, as a frustrated teenager with a well-thumbed copy of Peter Little and David English's *Start Here If You Want To Be A Racing Driver* on my bedside table, I was looking for exciting alternatives to motor racing. Scalextric wasn't going to cut it, even if squirting a bit of shampoo on the track taught me the finer nuances of throttle control, or pulling the tyres half-off allowed stunts like Ross Chastain's NASCAR last lap wall of death ride at Martinsville in 2022!

Like most of my generation, I spent a lot of time on my bike, setting up tracks on pavements, driveways and lawns. I didn't realise it at the time, but the variety of surfaces (especially the gravel!) taught me a sensitivity to grip and braking levels that probably benefits me to this day, not to mention a healthy appreciation of how competition can drive ever more impressive results! There was also a concrete path around part of our house that in theory made a perfect basis for time-trials. This path was so narrow, the only way around the corners without clobbering the house wall was to adopt a kind of Scandinavian flick, sliding the rear wheel wide. My parents weren't too impressed with the black tyre marks left as a result so I took it onto the local roads, which led to the kind of hair-raising encounters with the scenery expected of a thrill-seeking teen. I remember impaling my leg on a wooden stake in the hedge I'd cycled into. To be fair, I was distracted by a rather attractive local girl walking the other way. Of course, I had to pretend I was just fine when she came over to check, despite the blood leaking out of my left trouser leg. A far more serious impact was with the back of a parked Volvo Amazon. I was flat out, head down (no helmets in those days), and in the next instant, I was somersaulting through the air, somehow landing on my feet in front of said car! God knows how I was not injured, but the smashed rear light on the Volvo certainly damaged my pocket money income for many months.

Having reached the limit of my biking environment aged 13, I joined the Altrincham speed-skating club in response to a small advert in the local paper. Maybe inspired by my Dutch heritage, this seemed to be a cheap way to gain speed and actually race against other competitors. We are talking about short-track speed-skating here, something that eventually became an Olympic sport after Calgary in 1988 but was little-known before then. We skated anti-clockwise around a 111-metre oval ice track, marked out by wooden blocks. The radius of the corners was so tight that the g-force experienced was considerable: the skate blades were offset to the left of the boots to enable skaters to lean into the corner at the lowest possible angle (even if this offset made skating the straights a little challenging). This asymmetrical set-up approach was another piece of learning that would benefit me years later on the race track, but more of that later!

I spent hours preparing my skates on their jig, sharpening the edges for grip, adjusting the deepest point of the blade (influencing the forward position of my centre of gravity) and even investing in some leading-edge composite boot chassis that moulded themselves to a perfect fit with my feet (somewhat like the moulded seat inserts we use today in the race cars). Looking back, I can see there was so much of value that I took with me to motorsport and this learning wasn't restricted to the equipment: I also learned the basics of a racing line. An oval may be a simplistic lay out but a wide entry and exit of course minimises the speed loss through the corner. However, with other racers on track, that ideal approach led to ambitious lunges up the inside line, so very quickly I learned the awareness needed to defend or attack when six competitors all wanted the same piece of track. The rules of contact were somewhat ambiguous in those days, especially in the 'devil' races for non-finalists where contact was expected and encouraged; the speed-skating equivalent to a demolition derby!

I travelled with the Altrincham team all around the UK, from Nottingham to Richmond, from Birmingham to Peterborough, and learned that although the tracks may look similar on the surface, they all had their own nuances due to the concrete base, the freezing system, the ice preparation and whatever the ice had been used for just prior to the event. All these elements could impact how the skates ran in different parts of the track and make a difference to the optimal strategy. All great preparation for a life racing on four wheels!

I eventually turned 'senior' and raced against the adults, which was a major step up. I was pretty fit by that stage, cycling five miles to and from late-night training twice a week, and for some reason, my sprint starts on the ice were pretty effective. At my first senior race, I was leading into the second corner and with no one ahead, I misjudged the speed and lost it on the exit, sliding across the ice and smashing the barrier with my right foot, the heel of that skate slicing into my left thigh. The club could only afford to position barrier crash padding around the mid-corner, and my shunt just missed this, so it was no surprise my ankle broke on impact. The timing was terrible, as my dream at the time was to travel to the Calgary Olympics. Although I returned to speed-skating after my ankle recovered, I was never fully competitive again (largely a psychological issue) and in any case, now 17, I was learning how to drive!

ON THE ROAD

No surprise, Dad taught me how to drive. At the time, he had a second-generation 1600cc red Toyota Celica, which was actually pretty cool! Being rear-wheel-drive, it was a rewarding car to hustle along the A-roads of Derbyshire, but I was far from appreciating such things when I first got behind the wheel on the lanes near Altrincham. I'd spend weeks prior to this practicing launches and gear shifts up and down our short gravel drive. I could just about snatch second before I had to brake at the gate, but the loose surface was a definite bonus in terms of learning clutch and brake control!

Once out on the public roads, everything quickly felt very natural and I was encouraged to explore cornering lines, perfecting techniques like heel-and-toe and throttle use to help the car through the corners. I distinctly remember Dad excitedly yelling, "Keep your foot in!" as I rounded a helpfully-cambered curve near Knutsford in those early days. Of course, most of this learning had no place whatsoever in my forthcoming driving test; during the several formal driving lessons, my instructor spent a lot of time eradicating what he called 'bad habits' from my driving. I failed my first driving test; the given reason of 'undue hesitation' can only be explained as over-compensation after frequently being warned I was driving too fast in my lessons. I fared well at the second attempt and that summer my mate Phil and I took a two-week road trip around Scotland. There were some very long deserted sections of the A87 on the Isle of Skye where we could 'explore the full capabilities' of the Celica!

Having heard about our adventures, Dad sold the car soon after our return and replaced it with a rather bland Toyota Tercel, perhaps in a vain attempt to slow me down. Unfortunately, what did slow me down more effectively was a hedge *en route* from speed-skating training very late one winter night. That route runs between Mobberley and Hale, past Ashley, with a couple of railway bridge 'yumps' and several challenging corners and cambers. One such corner was a long left, awash with puddles on my way to the training session. On the way back, adopting similar speeds, I realised too late that those puddles had since frozen, as I ashamedly explained to Dad on the phone from the local farm. Thankfully, he was not overly concerned about the Tercel. "We can always get another car, we can't get another you!" was his philosophy, an attitude that is equally important for racing: ultimately, a car is just a tool and you can't be too precious about it, if driving fast is your goal.

It was clear I needed my own car to gain some sense of responsibility and this came in the form of a black 1978 Ford Fiesta 1300S. I'd pored over the 0-60mph times of the various choices and this was just about the quickest I could afford. I removed the bumpers, then filled and sprayed the rust holes on a windy day, so the car was mostly an unintentional but quite cool matte black. I fixed the head gasket after leaving a steam trail more impressive than the

Flying Scotsman, fitted Dad's old bucket racing seat and spent all my summer job earnings on a sports steering wheel and a cherry bomb exhaust. The car was then so loud that late at night Dad reckoned he could hear from around three miles away exactly which corners I was negotiating on my way home!

I suppose everyone's first car is remembered fondly and my Fiesta was no exception. It handled relatively well once I adjusted tyre pressures and straightened the Panhard rod I bent on a kerb whilst exploring the grip limits of the rear left! By this time, several mates had bought cars and with the impetuousness of youth (not to mention an unhealthy disregard for the law), we indulged in what were effectively road races, the longest being a sprint from Cheshire to a mate's house in Leicester, via Leek, Ashbourne and Derby. Coincidentally, the non-motorway section of the route was approximately the same length as the 1955 Targa Florio lap. Even if our cars were substantially less impressive than Stirling Moss's inspirational Mercedes 300SLR, it didn't stop us trying every trick and shortcut available to achieve 'victory', usually accompanied by eighties rock soundtracks blasting from the oversized speakers crudely mounted into our respective parcel shelves. Things did get out of hand one day all the way down south on the M25 when Phil, driving an Austin Maestro, was so determined to block my slipstream pass, he pulled out when we had an overlap, my front left bumper catching his rear right. After a heart-stopping moment, we both gathered it together, thankfully with no harm done, but there was no doubt we were pushing our luck.

Around this time, I went to watch a relatively minor race meeting at Oulton Park, accompanied by my mum. Her first car was a very cool Austin-Healey 'Frogeye' Sprite and she'd always supported Dad in the paddock and pit lane when he'd been racing in the 1950s. We were standing at the entry to Old Hall corner and could see the drivers working the wheel into the apex. "I know I could do that!" were the words I said to her, and that summer I convinced her I should attend a half-day single-seater session at the Team Touraco race school at Cadwell Park. This is one of the most challenging circuits in the UK, often described as the 'mini-Nürburgring' (very prescient for my later racing ambitions) with its tight twists, elevation changes and yes, a jump! As we drove in, I just couldn't believe how narrow the track was: I thought we were on an approach road until I saw the green-and-white kerbing! The day was fantastic, even if I missed a few gears thanks to inexperience with a right-handed shifter on the Van Diemen Formula Ford. It truly whet my appetite and in 1987, I resolved to work the summer job hard (as a furniture delivery driver) to fund a five-day residential course at Cadwell.

This course was a turning point for me: Team Touraco, operated by the fantastically mad Graham Glew, didn't adopt the same 'production line' approach as most other racing schools of the time. They believed in taking drivers to the limit and beyond, which is truly the only way to maximise your capabilities. For example, we'd learn to 'work a bend', focussing on a single section of the track until we had it nailed. Can you imagine a racing school today allowing a flat-out approach to Park corner at the end of Cadwell's main straight, with one instructor standing trackside by the turning-in point and another standing on the apex, waving his arms energetically to encourage full throttle and a smidge of oversteer at that point? I can't stress enough how valuable this experience was: some folks never approach that limit in years of racing. We did the same at the much slower hairpin, acquiring the skills to induce controlled oversteer on the brakes and maintain it with the throttle. Instruction and examination alongside Graham in an Escort XR3i was followed by the major highlight, a back-to-back session with Kelvin Burt, British F3 champion and Formula 1 test driver, but then still a Formula First driver. If you're thinking back-to-back meant Kelvin set a lap and we had to beat it, remember Team Touraco was not your average racing school. Back-to-back literally meant driving directly behind Kelvin at full racing speed! I distinctly remember being glued to his gearbox around those laps, watching him watch me in his mirror, and being utterly convinced this was my future.

At the end of the course, Team Touraco awarded a prize for the most promising driver: a testing contract within their Formula First team. I'm proud to say I won that prize and spent several days over the next year pounding around Cadwell, working to perfect my driving and my understanding of set-up with a dedicated engineer. Reality struck however, when I learned the next step progressing to the race team would require a budget of some £30,000. I was on my way to university and in no position to find that kind of money, so I had to park my ambitions and find other routes to satisfy my 'speedlust'.

My next flirtation with competitive driving that summer was at long-time friend Jon's house back in Cheshire. His parents owned a field with a small pond halfway down one side, and they were very relaxed about us turning it into a rally course. Jon had a signal-orange Mk2 Escort MOT failure that provided supremely valuable experience in terms of developing our driving skills in a low-grip environment. We used garden canes to mark out a variety of courses that quickly became slick with mud. Experimental methods were tried to reduce lap time, the most effective being a passenger in the rear seat slamming themselves sideways against the interior as the driver turned into each corner, instantly provoking oversteer just at the right moment to get the car rotated! There was no prize except bragging rights for my 31-second lap record, unbeaten even when one fool decided to try a shortcut between the pond and the hedge. That lap came to an abrupt end short of the finish line. The resulting extreme negative camber on the front looked cool, but really wasn't a very effective tweak so the car was abandoned in the field soon after. As the Escort had given us so much, it was actually quite emotional to see it a year later, sunk down to its axles in the long grass, with weeds growing up through the bonnet.

Following Dad's advice to focus on my studies, in October 1988 I'd enrolled in the automotive industrial design degree course at Coventry University. I figured it would give me a deeper insight into the workings and responses of a car and make me a better, more sensitive driver as a result. In fact, it gave me more than that: aside from fairly intensive mechanical engineering and production engineering courses, we had access to a wind tunnel, giving me insights that are valuable even to this day. Design genius Adrian Newey is allegedly able to 'see air' flowing over a race car and that's not a far-fetched claim: understanding how airflow and pressure interact with the surfaces of a vehicle (or multiple vehicles together) is complex but very logical. It's the compromises, particularly between downforce and drag, that really make a difference to a race car, and at that time of limited computing power there was no substitute for the hands-on hours I spent in the wind tunnel.

Whilst at Coventry, I dabbled in some road rallies organised by the university motor club, but these were nothing like the overnight events Dad had contested around 30 years before. All routes had to be reported to the local police, speeds were obviously controlled and the events were really glorified treasure hunts, without the benefit of a sat-nav of course. When my navigator struggled even to direct me out of Coventry city centre one foggy winter evening, I gave it up. I decided to surprise my parents by driving home to Cheshire unannounced, and like so many before me, I stuffed the car on roads I knew like the back of my hand, just a few miles from their house. Missing my braking point in the foggy darkness, I crashed so heavily into the vicarage wall on a 90-degree left that the floor buckled under my feet. I'm sure I was saved by the bucket seat, and my knees by the smaller sports steering wheel. I remember hearing the tinkling of broken glass in the silence afterwards, wiggling toes and fingers to be sure I was uninjured. After yet another farmhouse phone call, Dad arrived and curiously told me to empty the car of my belongings, which turned out to be a good idea: the next day when we went to recover the car, someone had smashed the windows and taken whatever was left.

Predictably but sadly, the Fiesta was a write-off and so I had no choice but to find a cheap alternative: a Chrysler Avenger that eventually turned out to be stolen! It ran well even if when I changed gear, "something black came out of the exhaust and hit my windscreen" according to a following friend. The car was actually quite fun to drive, especially in the snowy lanes of Derbyshire. It was built like a tank and it was possible to use the snow banks to arrest an over-enthusiastic tail slide! Its robustness proved its worth at 6am on the M1, when I was involved in a four-car pile-up with a Jaguar, a BMW and a Ford Escort. We'd stopped for a queue, except for the Escort that hardly braked before smashing into the BMW. Even though I couldn't open the doors of the Avenger afterwards, my pedal bike in the boot was unharmed! The weirdest thing? I had met the guy in the Escort at a party two weeks before in Birmingham! What are the chances?

And so onto budget car number three for 1990, a very mediocre old silver Honda Accord, that successfully carried my friend Alan and I on a road trip to the Hungarian Grand Prix, to watch Thierry Boutsen hold off Ayrton Senna and Nelson Piquet. The only trackside refreshments in those days were watermelons! That night, after a visit to the aptly-named Black Hole nightclub in Budapest, we climbed into our Honda parked in a dark side-street, only to find some joker had moved the steering wheel to the left side of the dashboard! In our less than alert condition, it took us a while to realise this wasn't our Accord, even if my key had opened it! Our journey home was somewhat circuitous, including an interesting 'race' back through the twists of the Italian Alps, our local 'opponent' diving off the road behind us, only to reappear in front a few clicks later! He eventually flagged us down to explain he could see petrol was leaking from our lost fuel cap.

Honestly, in response to the abuse we'd thrown at the car, that was the least of our concerns and with a dire lack of remaining brake pad material, it was amazing we made it back to the UK without further incident. The Honda quietly expired in the blizzards of the next winter, but not before several of us had a great deal of Scandinavian hand-brake fun one night in the local supermarket carpark when we saw the white stuff coming down. For some reason, the police didn't believe our reasoning that we were all shopping at 3am. When the several feet of snow melted, pretty much all that remained of the Honda was four tyres and the gaffer tape that had been holding it together!

With no funds available to go racing through 1990, I had to be satisfied helping Sue, a friend of the family, who was just starting to race a relatively standard Alfasud. We'd had several 'Sud and Sprint road cars and always appreciated their perky boxer engines and precise handling (largely attributed to the engine's low centre of gravity and the inboard front brake discs reducing the unsprung weight in the suspension, as I learned). After a season running near the back of the field, Sue was kind enough to reward me with my first race opportunity at Donington Park GP circuit in October, in borrowed kit, to see how I'd get on in what frankly was a less-than-competitive car. As they say, what comes around comes around... unless it gets stuck in the gravel at what has since been named Fogarty Esses. Being one of the very few times she ever attended one of my races, Mum was on the pit wall and was not impressed with my fading brakes excuse.

Nevertheless, the experience clearly re-awoke something in Dad, who soon after made a proposition to me: as I didn't have sufficient savings, if he bought an old 'Sud race car and I paid for the consumables along the way (fuel, tyres, repairs and rebuilds and so on), perhaps we could go racing ourselves in the 1991 Chris Knott Insurance Alfa Romeo Championship? This was the stuff of dreams and I signed up without a second thought!

That winter, I got kitted out at the wonderful old Demon Tweeks racewear shop in Tattenhall. In the garden shed, I hand-sprayed my new helmet with the blue-and-yellow tear-drop design I kept for many years after, using a length of garden hose as a make-shift breathing tube, emerging red-faced and choking, much to my parents' amusement!

JOIN THE CLUB

B eing trackside the previous season gave us a good appreciation of the quick cars and drivers in the Alfa Romeo Championship, and we found a red 'Sud prepared and raced that year by a chap called Colin, in Class C where some level of performance modification was allowed (but without any change to the original steel body), the cars running on grooved tyres. Class C raced alongside a variety of other classes, including the much more heavily modified Class A and B cars running on slicks, with glass-fibre aerodynamic modifications and considerably faster lap times. Things didn't start well with a pretty big pre-season testing accident, when a front brake pad jumped out of the calliper. As you'll read further in the 5am Superstitions & Premonitions chapter, there was a very strange paranormal aspect to this accident, but fortunately at least we were able to straighten the car ready for the first race in April.

The Class C pacesetter that year and in previous years was a green 'Sud driven by Ted Pearson, who clearly became our benchmark. With our fairly basic engine, we just couldn't keep up with him on the straights so it felt like a huge victory when, in June, we managed to pass Ted at a soaking wet race at the very quick Castle Combe (pre-chicanes format). Rain is a great leveller of equipment, but over the final laps, I saw Ted gaining on me along Dean Straight. Coming into Camp corner for the final time, with the finish line in sight, I was so determined to hold the lead I left my braking insanely late. Somewhere there is a trackside video of our car slewing into a lurid slide through most of the corner, my foot hard down on the throttle, just about pulling it straight for our first class victory! On the podium, I felt like I'd arrived, albeit somewhat late, aged 21!

We won again in September at Castle Combe, this time in the dry, having missed a few races to install a new engine, which unfortunately then blew up at the next race in October at Mallory Park. Here starteth the lesson: chasing performance in motorsport is expensive and frustrating! Nevertheless, a Class E competitor, Ian Connell, very kindly lent me his Alfetta GTV, a quite different animal that allowed us a third-in-class finish at the next race at Snetterton. It's generous folks like Ian who make racing such a pleasure, and our friendship continues to this day.

Later in October, Graham Bloor, an old racing friend of Dad's, was racing a beautiful Frogeye Sprite (very similar to my mum's first car) at an HSCC event at Snetterton. Graham was looking for a co-driver and somehow he was convinced I could fill that seat. We arrived in Norfolk, me with a certain amount of trepidation. I should not have worried: the HSCC crowd were very welcoming and their manners on track were exemplary, allowing me to focus on driving the car. The Sprite's little 948cc engine was fully race-prepared and was pretty difficult to manoeuvre off track compared to the 'Sud. The guys who were there to help Graham were shaking their heads as I kangarooed down the pit line in the cramped cockpit, but to Dad's amusement, they did a double-take when they glanced at their stop watches after I got on with it out on track.

I count the Sprite as a key step in my race-driving apprenticeship for the simple reason that it gave me a reference for what a perfect set-up feels like. It was easily possible to steer the car with the throttle through the long high-speed corners such as Riches or Coram, setting up a thrilling four-wheel drift, but equally it was precise and direct in the low-speed corners, allowing me to carry speed and compensate for the relatively low power. Even a tricky corner like the Bombhole was straightforward in this car, despite the entry dip initially causing alarming understeer on turn in, before the rising on-camber exit built the grip back up. It was a confidence-inspiring experience and we qualified ahead of the other two identical Sprites, after which Graham kindly applied the ethos, "He who sets the qualifying pace takes the start." In the race, I was mixing it with Lotus Elans and MGs, lapping around three seconds faster than the other Sprites and probably pushing too hard, which led to a small gearbox oil leak. That didn't slow us down and neither did the gear knob parting company with the lever, leaving me to change gear with the remaining stump that left a bloody gash on my palm to remind me of a fantastic race. The race-craft learning for me was meteoric; the cars around me were so different, I could begin to understand their strengths and weaknesses around the lap and adapt my tactics accordingly.

Unfortunately, this learning didn't transfer to the start of the 1992 season, when we returned with our Class C Alfasud, determined to complete the whole championship. We had another new engine, this time built by man-bear Dave Litchfield: he would install the boxer engine by carrying it on his chest on a trolley under the car! The hope was that the car would be on the pace with Ted even in the dry, but achieving this also allowed us to run with some of the quicker cars in Class A or B. At Mallory Park in April, running behind the slick-shod Class A Alfa 75 of Clive Hodgkin, I felt he was holding me up and rashly took a dive down the inside into Gerards, the fast right hander at the end of the pit straight. Braking a fraction after Clive, my grooved tyres vainly searched for grip and I ploughed sideways into the gravel, flipping the car in slow-motion and coming to rest upside down.

Oddly, I was relatively calm, maybe because it wasn't the first time I'd had to crawl out of an inverted car: my old field-rallying school-friend Jon had provided me with that initiation when he lost control of his Renault 12 ferrying me home from school. At least this time, there was no carful of fishing tackle to obstruct my exit! However, I had invited my Swiss girlfriend to watch at Mallory and she was certainly not calm, having been spectating directly opposite the crash site. Thankfully, little harm was done apart from a cracked windscreen (yes, a 'consumable' for which I was liable!), a few dents to the roof panel and a few more sizeable dents to my pride. It may sound obvious, but a proper understanding of the capabilities of the immediate competition is a key part of any success in life, whether sporting or business. My Mallory accident was the last time I made that ignorant mistake. On the other hand, it certainly wasn't the last time I crashed in my racing career!

In May 1992, our little Alfa Romeo Championship supported the British Touring Cars at Snetterton. Watching the likes of Will Hoy, John Cleland, Andy Rouse, David Leslie and other heroes on the track I'd just driven was the first time I realistically began to seriously consider there might be a path for me in that direction. Unfortunately, I disgraced myself by failing to spot a yellow flag in qualifying and after the subsequent penalty was applied, I had to drive through from the back of the grid. We climbed up to third before being black-flagged due to oil smoke from a blown seal. At least I saw that flag...

In August, we arrived at Castle Combe with the engine pulling 150bhp on the dyno and ready to fight, but as the qualifying time sheet showed, our car was 'not seen'. An overzealous scrutineer had decided that the race seat being bolted (not welded) into our car was not to regulation (incorrect), and we could not expect to race 'at his circuit' like that. He proceeded to karate-kick the seat until the mounts broke. We completely missed qualifying whilst we had the seat mounts welded in the garage just outside the circuit, consequently having to start the race at the back of the grid. We fought through to second in class and set an encouraging fastest lap over half a second quicker than Ted. Oh and those welded seat mounts broke during the race...

As the season progressed, we realised there was only so far we could go with the Class C car. Things came to a head when, at Donington in September, qualifying was cancelled due to fog. The grid was a randomly decided by the championship coordinator and, with a mix of capabilities up front, we made it as far as braking for Redgate corner before being punted up the rear by another competitor who would usually have been way behind us.

A discussion with Dave Litchfield followed: he had built a heavily modified Class B 'Sud, owned and raced by a chap called Munro. Dave encouraged me to test the car at Mallory and the car did not disappoint. It was super light-weight thanks to composite body panels (and a few non-critical rust holes!), with enormous Yokohama motorcycle racing side-car slick tyres on the front, balanced by somewhat harder and narrower Avons on the rear that allowed the car to rotate into the corners like nothing I'd driven before. We ran laps three seconds quicker than the pace Munro set as a reference. We could see there was even more potential in the car and so, fuelled by dreams of big things, we did a deal right there, affordable only by Dave sharing driving duties with me in 1993 in return for his race preparation services.

It was at this point I realised the trick Dad had pulled with the 'you pay for the consumables' deal when we had bought the Class C car. He sold that car for more than he originally paid, thanks to our success developing it. As I was responsible only for consumables, I had nothing to sell but for a few part-worn tyres. A hard lesson but a good one!

Sharing the car with Dave was not only a breakthrough financial solution, but also a great help technically. We'd been developing the car ourselves and learning a lot about tyre pressures, dampers, camber, caster, toe, anti-roll bars and ride heights, basically all you can find in excellent handbooks such as *Performance Handling* by Don Alexander that was my bedtime reading at the time. Having Dave on board also improved our reliability, and in club racing that means less laying on your back in the paddock mud, trying to fix the car on the trailer.

By this time, I'd been at Coventry University for a couple of years, and in the third year I secured an industrial placement with Dow Automotive in northern Switzerland (a choice that may have been motivated by my then girlfriend's location in Winterthur). Dow offered me a job and I went back to Switzerland after I qualified at Coventry in 1992 (where I stayed awake for a ridiculous 56 hours to complete my final project; great practice, I suppose, for later endurance racing challenges). I didn't know it at the time but Dow would play a large part in my racing career.

Living in Switzerland gave me the opportunity to learn how to ski properly. It was a steep learning curve amongst folks who had skied almost as soon as they could walk, but to be honest, I had no choice: most winter weekends, every one of my local friends disappeared to the slopes. In any case, I recommend skiing for any race driver, as it requires very similar skills of balance, grip management, foresight and, let's be honest, bravery (or foolhardiness depending on your talent and choice of skiing buddies). I had my fair share of shunts in the mountains, long before helmets were *de rigeur*, probably the worst being intimate contact with a piste marker pole as a result of attempting to shortcut a hairpin. The impact resulted in a spectacular butterfly of crimson blood on the snow as I lay blissfully unconscious. On a positive note, that pole altered the profile of my nose, I'd like to think for the better!

Motor racing being illegal in Switzerland (since the 1955 Le Mans disaster), I had no choice but to fly back to UK to race the new 'Sud in the 1993 Alfa Romeo Championship and also in the BRSCC Italian Intermarque Championship that shared the same events (racing against Ferraris, Lancias and other cool stuff). Fortunately, I had some Dow customer responsibilities in the UK so the travel burden wasn't too punitive for my own wallet. Coincidentally, Yokohama Europe was located very close to where I worked in the neighbourhood of Kreuzlingen. In spite of the funny looks, I would occasionally carry two slick tyre 'test samples' back with me to the UK as plane luggage. Dad would meet me in his Volvo 240GLT with its cavernous boot for all our kit, towing the race car up to the terminal at whatever airport was closest to the race meeting.

On one return trip, there were even more funny looks from the Swiss as I was carrying an empty beer can, some coat hanger wire and a tube of mysterious paste. The older Volvo 240 I was also running at the time had a holed exhaust and of course, in Switzerland, nobody but an English guy would consider trying to repair it themselves. When my neighbours saw my legs sticking out from under the car, they gathered around thinking something dreadful had happened! My Volvo also had a piece of scaffolding tube as a replacement drive shaft and a small piece of black insulation tape obscuring a particularly persistent dashboard warning light! Anything to save money for racing...

The lightweight Litchfield 'Sud proved to be an absolute weapon: our 1700cc engine was one of the smallest in Class A, but we took pole position, the win and fastest lap at Silverstone in March. Dave then achieved precisely the same at Brands Hatch and again at Mallory Park. As is always the case, especially outside one-make racing, the car makes a much greater contribution to success than the driver! Dave continued pushing development of the engine, now bored out to 1836cc. Ted Pearson had uprated his car to Class A and we had ex-F2 driver Kim Mather to contest with in a 3000cc ex-Italian Alfa 75 touring car, who brought a whole new level of 'pro-driver' aggression to the party. There's a great picture of our 'Sud leading Kim at Donington, my inside wheel just tickling the blue-and-white apex kerbs of the chicane, and his outside wheels fully inside that same kerb! Dad was really unhappy with his bumping and bashing and the resulting bodywork damage, but in hindsight it was a great education for me ahead of the more serious competition to come.

Chris Snowdon joined us at Donington GP circuit in June with his yellow beast of a 3300cc GTV6. In qualifying, Kim, Chris and I were separated by 17 hundredths of a second. Although we went even faster in the race, our new engine exploded spectacularly on the run up to McLeans. The mangled conrod that had punched a hole in our engine block was later repurposed by Dad as a unique trophy for the club! In all honesty, it was this that inspired me years later to spray a failed starter-motor with gold paint, mount it on a polished wooden base and present it to Aston Martin's Head of Motorsport, after it cost us the 2018 Nürburgring 24 hours race. I think he saw the funny side but I'm not sure that award will be found anywhere in Aston Martin's trophy cabinet!

Back to 1993, Dave Litchfield showed his fabulous character by taking full responsibility for the engine failure, and refitting our old 150bhp spec engine for his next race at Cadwell, impressively taking second behind Kim. Between us, this was the more or less the maximum we could achieve. We sneaked another win in October at Cadwell Park in Chris's absence (with Kim finishing an unusual sixth), doubling up with victory in the Italian Intermarque.

1994 saw a rule change that meant we'd run in Class B, bringing different competition in the form of Nick Humphrey's Alfa 33, even if our raised-compression engine and new tyres still allowed us to scrap with the Class A cars. These now included Roberto Giordanelli's curiously rapid GTA and Chris Snowdon's GTV6 amongst others. Our 'Sud now made use of some huge inboard front brake discs that actually were the lowest point under the car, meaning I had to be wary of clobbering them by straddling high apex kerbs. We also decided to implement some of the aerodynamic learning I'd picked up in Coventry and fabricated a plywood 'splitter' to provide more downforce at the front of the car in the higher speed corners. Crucially, this device extended as far back under the car as possible, impeded mainly by the position of those massive brake discs. The main disadvantage of the splitter was that people in the paddock kept standing on it by accident, hence the rather unsightly yellow hazard tape we stuck all over it!

At Pembrey in June, with its high-speed Honda Curve or Dibeni Bend into Paddock, the splitter did its job and we lapped just five-hundredths of a second slower than Chris's Class A winning car, before a stone holed our radiator leading to a DNF. A wonderful member of the Welsh public actually lent us their road car radiator, allowing us to win the following Italian Intermarque race! Over this season, we either won Class B races or endured a DNF due to mechanical gremlins.

1995 was really our year, taking both the Italian Intermarque and the Alfa Romeo Championships, the latter with Class B wins at Thruxton, Cadwell Park (twice), Snetterton, Oulton Park (twice) and Donington. This last win was later nulled due to an exasperating disqualification. I had passed Nick's 33 on the inside at Redgates, who then smashed into the back of our 'Sud at the chicane, pushing me wide and retaking the lead. I was infuriated and as a result, I didn't see a yellow flag as I re-passed Nick at Redgates. The learning, of course, was to always remain calm, whatever occurs during the race. In any case, karma caught up with Nick the next week at Oulton Park, when his car was off the pace, his trick engine underperforming apparently 'due to ingesting glass'. As Dad pointed out, this hazard could have been eliminated by avoiding driving into the car in front!

We encountered a strange phenomenon at Oulton Park in August, this time on a technical front. The car was pulling to the left on the straights, despite no damage or anything misaligned, and we seemed to be down on power in qualifying. We'd been running an old set of the Yokohama motorcycle side car tyres on the front, and when we fitted a new set for the race, the problem disappeared. It was only when we were back home that the mystery was solved: we measured the circumference of the two old tyres with a high-tech length of string and found they were a couple of centimetres different! In discussion with Yokohama, it transpired that nobody (except us) ran these tyres on a common axle: motorcycle side-cars' wheels of course have no common axle, so variations in circumference between tyres was no big deal. In our case, the mismatch was working the differential on the straights, sapping power, and of course pulling the car off course on acceleration. From that point on we were very careful to match tyres on the 'Sud.

If you'd like to get an impression of how well that car handled, check out Chris Snowdon's on-board footage (Cadwell Park Onboard uploaded on YouTube in 2009 by AleXcr_86). We had so much front-end grip, we could pass Chris's GTV6 around the outside into the Hairpin, although oil on the track in the following laps made braking for that corner somewhat challenging, as the clouds of smoke from my left-front lock ups show. An article at the time entitled *Advanced Braking To Win* used a cover photo of exactly this moment; I might have suggested a different image!

Our success in the 1995 season was a turning point for me. I'd moved back to UK with the intent to take my racing more seriously, climbing onto the bottom of the housing ladder in the summer. Inspired by Tarquini, Simoni and Warwick racing the Alfa Romeo 155s in the British Touring Car Championship (BTCC), I picked up the phone and rather naïvely called Prodrive to explain why I felt I deserved a shot. There was a polite silence (during which I suspect they were quietly laughing on mute) and they advised me to prove myself in one-make racing, where the winning difference is to a great extent more about the drivers than the cars. TOCA was running the BTCC in the 1990s and their support races were the highest-profile option in

UK, but I didn't have access to the £30,000 required for a competitive season in Fiestas (the entry level TOCA Championship), not to mention the further cost of buying the Fiesta race car in the first place. After enduring a horribly frustrating year out of racing in 1996, I sold my house, moved into the Surrey two-up two-down of new girlfriend Kim (not possible to confuse her with Kim Mather, I can assure you) and signed up for 1997 Fiesta season! It wasn't the smartest or most prudent financial decision at the time, but looking back, it was pivotal.

GETTING SERIOUS

In my head, I had conceived a five-year plan at the start of 1997, which would culminate in a BTCC drive. The Super Touring cars of the time were a huge draw, a real golden age in racing history. With drivers like Jason Plato making the jump from the TOCA support races of the Renault Spider Cup in 1996 to the Williams Renault touring car in 1997, I could clearly see the possibilities.

The plan was to be launched with the Ford Credit Fiesta Championship, followed by a pathway through the Vauxhall Vectra Sri V6 Challenge, both of which were part of the TOCA package supporting BTCC around the UK, offering great live and televised visibility for drivers and sponsors. The intent was to spend two years in each championship, a first learning year and a second winning year. Winning the Vectra Challenge also carried the dream prize of a funded BTCC drive the following year, an immense attraction.

I approached one Fiesta team owner, Colin Stancombe at Oulton Park and had a chat about racing together. This ultimately proved to be a mistake as will become evident. I was working for Dow Automotive with Ford in Essex at this time. Colin's team was based relatively close to me which I thought a good thing, but as I recall, he was running six Fiestas including his own and their results in 1996 were only average.

I wasn't sure if I could make the winning difference but my budget limitations meant the top teams were out of the question. In any case, we struck a deal and at the first Fiesta race in March at Donington, having been out of a seat for a year, I was elated to finish second, just ahead of the incumbent Fiesta champion Gareth Downing!

One-make racing like this was certainly a further education for me. The first lesson was to take qualifying a lot more seriously than I had needed to in the Alfa, for two reasons. First, the field is divided into three types of drivers: those at the front who are fast and don't crash, those at the back who drive too slowly to crash, and those in the midfield who crash frequently, mostly into each other, as they attempt to drive too fast for their capabilities. This last category is a real danger zone and I learned the hard way the importance of qualifying ahead of this pack of animals! One such driver was eventually excluded from the championship mid-season for appalling contact with our car and numerous others.

The second learning was the tiny differences between success and failure. The top ten in qualifying could be separated by a tenth of a second over a lap. The Fiesta Zetec engines only produced around 90bhp so it was critical to maximise the track, to carry speed through the corners and to stay in touch with cars ahead to take advantage of their slipstream. A missed gear or a slight lock up and you were back in that mid-field danger zone. Amongst that chaos, there was very little chance to recover a leading position.

I'm not going to dwell much further on the 1997 season, simply because more podium results never came. After several mid-season setbacks, including a failed hub at Thruxton, a puncture at Oulton Park, a drive shaft failure at Croft and a big shunt at Brands Hatch's Druids corner (courtesy of close competitor Neal Gordon), a series of fourth- and fifth-place finishes at Knockhill, Donington and Snetterton (with fastest lap for the first time) allowed me to finish a creditable sixth in the championship, behind several more experienced Fiesta drivers. However, my relationship with Colin deteriorated (as is detailed more fully in the 8am People Power chapter). I should have learned from team mate Alan Morrison, who left for another team mid-season. I resolved to switch teams for 1998 rather than waste any more of my dwindling funds with a team that I felt did not allow me to be fully competitive.

Meeting Mark Fish not far from Harlow over the winter was a breath of fresh air. He had successfully run one-make race cars before but not Fiestas, and he was open to the challenge. He committed to run just two cars which appealed to me; I wanted to bring together all our experience with maximum effect, without the distraction of dealing with multiple other drivers. Our first meeting was almost derailed when Kim mentioned to Mark that I was something of a 'collectomaniac'. It's true I did like to collect things, but Mark heard 'kleptomaniac'! After we left, I could imagine him discretely counting his spanners! Another big draw at Mark Fish Motorsport was Bob Friend, at that stage an apprentice mechanic, but clearly already destined for great things. He has since gone on to become Team Manager at Jota Sport, one of the most successful modern sports car racing teams.

Colin was livid when I took my 1997 car to Mark Fish. He tried to change all the suspension settings but Mark wasn't fooled. In any case, I had kept all my set-up notes. After selling that car, Mark sourced a brand-new low-mileage ex-rental Fiesta from the Channel Islands and meticulously built it up to championship regulations. We spent several evenings discussing how to maximise its performance, one of which, inspired by the paintless bodies of the Silver Arrows in the 1950s, was to run unpainted bumpers to save weight. Funny how the Formula 1 cars of today have only recently come back around to this idea! All the ingredients were in place for a good season and indeed we were in contention for victory throughout. To stay true to the intent of this book, I'll only include here the season's highlights that brought invaluable experiences worth sharing.

Thruxton stands out, as it was the first time I'd led a Fiesta race, a position that of course requires a new skill of controlling the race, driving just fast enough to maintain the lead but not so fast as to destroy the tyres or make a more catastrophic error. Thruxton is a super-fast track that I love, a typically windy airfield location. Slipstreaming is a key feature there, and on that day, leading the field through Brooklands up to the Club chicane, the speed differential of the following cars in my draft meant that when I hit the brakes, even as late as I dared, I was punted off as I turned in and quickly found myself well down in 12th place. A recovery to fifth was small consolation and the incident brought me to the first of many post-race Clerk of the Course meetings that frequently delayed our homeward journey on Sunday evenings.

Mark had signed a second driver, Michael, who brought a fabulously filthy sense of humour to the team. I don't think I will ever unsee Michael standing in the doorway of our race truck, race-suit open to the waist, abusing Mark's bottle of yoghurt drink in his fist with accompanying lewd sound effects! By his own admission, Michael wasn't so serious about his racing as I was; not really that interested in finding the essential last couple of tenths in the set-up. At Knockhill, we knew we needed to draft each other in qualifying and arranged it so I'd get the draft from Michael after Clark corner, along the Railway Straight, so he could then pull right to let me take the line into the hairpin. The problem was I caught him early into Clark and he then spun, taking us both off!

Kim and I had borrowed a motorhome for this event and there was a torrential overnight storm which damaged our awning. Sometime in the small hours we were awoken by the arrival of two local guys, who proceeded to try to put up their tent. In the morning, we found them, one wrapped in the flysheet and the other in the ground sheet, tent poles scattered around! Hardy folk these Scots, although I suspect their beer coats kept them warm!

It was still raining when our Fiesta took to the track. Frustratingly, I suffered a faulty fuse that caused the windscreen wipers to malfunction, the wiper blades frozen a few inches above their resting position. I found out afterwards they had wanted to black flag me for this, but Mark had argued it was the driver's choice to continue, which I did. That meant I had to loosen my seat belts (absolutely not recommended!) to peer through the narrow strip of clear windscreen just above the motionless wiper blades, using a bit of muscle-memory to steer through the corners. It wasn't so bad in the streaming rain, but when cars ahead ran wide and spattered my windscreen with Knockhill mud, I could hardly see a thing. We finished sixth like that but not before a multi-car 'pile up' at Taylors hairpin delayed matters. This resulted in a protest from Neal Gordon, his car having been at the front of the pile-up, another naughty-boy meeting with the Clerk of the Course and over the next months, numerous letters to a Tribunal, but finally the result stood. Not a side of racing I'd anticipated, nor one I liked.

The next race at Snetterton was hot and dry. My mate Phil turned up in a TVR Cerbera and set fire to the paddock grass with its hot exhaust, prompting a few minutes of panic! On the first lap, I was able to jump up to third place passing two cars under braking into the Esses, setting me up to scrap for second place once again with Neal Gordon. Ultimately, I managed to come out on top. That podium was a key moment because it allowed me to get noticed by Mark Lemmer, team principal at Barwell Motorsport, who were running TOCA Vectras at that time. Pat Martin, (an engineer at Barwell and friend of my team mate Michael's), introduced me and this opened the door to an end of season test and couple of Vectra races to evaluate my performance.

Racing two quite different cars at the same event is not straightforward. The Vectra was so different to the Fiesta, not only in terms of the power and speed of the 215bhp 2.5L V6, but also in terms of the chassis and the way the Vectra's limited-slip differential worked. My first Vectra test at Oulton Park was an unmitigated disaster. First, I really struggled to input enough revs on the downshift to overcome the diff., and this soon put me into the gravel at Lodge corner. No damage done until the recovery crew failed to notice a buried steel hawser in the gravel which pulled off the front bumper as they dragged me out backwards.

Rejoining the test after repairs were completed over a rainy lunchtime, the track had dried and I was determined to make amends. The Vectras ran quite a soft compound Dunlop slick which really only gave one great lap of performance before deteriorating, so I was pushing pretty hard as I approached Old Hall corner for the first time. What I had not seen, owing to the fact the pit lane exit shortcuts Old Hall, was the remaining puddle at the apex, which spat me directly off over the wet grass and into the tyre wall, bouncing the car over onto its roof. It's a great credit to Mark and the Barwell crew that they didn't lose faith in me; in fact they helped to restore my own faith in myself. I was glad to reward them with fourth place at the flag, my enduring memory being the battle with Vectra regular Dave Pinkney, who crowded me so close to the pit wall that all the crews had to hurriedly snatch away their pit boards as we whipped past.

The last race of the Fiesta season was a double-header at Silverstone, where I would again additionally pilot the Vectra. Qualifying was wet and at the brilliant Bridge corner (now sadly consigned to history), I lost the back of the Fiesta on my first flying lap, lazily sliding into the tyres on the exit. I was able to bring it back to the pits where Mark (Fish) and Bob manhandled the front wing and bonnet back into more or less their correct position, just in time for me to go again. I was pretty fired up and perhaps as a result of this, we snatched pole for Race 1 from eventual 1998 champion Alan Morrison. For Race 2, we qualified second, just seven-thousands of a second behind him. Such is Fiesta racing!

In Race 1, we led from start to... a gearbox failure on the penultimate lap! A loose bolt had dropped into the selector mechanism and I was gearless, cruising to a frustrated halt directly in front of the pits. Race 2 was better: with a rocket start, some careful tyre management and judicious defending, I finally took my first Fiesta win. It was bitter-sweet standing on top of the old Silverstone podium at Woodcote (great view from up there by the way): I was on the top step but Alan Morrison was crowned champion and I had only finished fourth in the final standings. I literally had to run between Fiesta and Vectra that day, taking the Vauxhall to sixth place for Barwell, my mind already on the 1999 season.

VECTRAPEZE ACT

Progression to Vectras with the necessary front-running team required a budget around £100,000 (at least this did not require the additional purchase of the race car). Fortunately, with our good results in the Fiesta, I was able to secure sufficient backing from three companies, Dexter Corporation, Byline Group and Dow Automotive. It meant for the first time in my driving career I was not paying for my racing. How I achieved this is detailed in the 12pm Show Me The Money chapter.

Although I intended to drive with Barwell, there was a distraction over the winter in the form of a competition, organised by racer Tim Sugden, the prize being a fully-funded drive in the same 1999 Vectra Championship! It was a clever and far-sighted scheme, with applicants paying to participate in each round, including media-style interviews, driving trials up at Elvington and physical fitness assessments. I'm sure I was not the fittest of all the contenders there, but perhaps I was the most determined not to lose. My distance running style does tend to make me look more exhausted than I am; embarrassingly, not long ago, a lady pulled up next to me when I was jogging and asked me if I needed a lift! Nevertheless, that day I made it through to the final ten in the competition. The final round was held at Croft circuit, but there, evaluating me from the passenger seat in a Vectra race car, Tim felt I was altogether too relaxed, particularly not liking my habit of holding onto the gear stick between shifts. I should have known he wouldn't appreciate me telling him one-handed steering never slowed Archie Scott Brown in the 1950s, and needless to say I didn't win the competition. Alan Morrison did, but ironically his prize Vectra was not that quick when we first hit the track the next season. It was only later in the season after my brakes overheated and I hit him in the door at Donington's Melbourne hairpin that he got a new body shell and was immediately on the pace. You're welcome, my Northern Irish friend!

My team mates at Barwell were quick: MGF champion James Rhodes and Vectra regular Jason Yeomans. Sharing set-up data would be a tremendous advantage for all of us. Of course, in Fiestas, we'd had various options to optimise damper settings, geometry, ride heights and so on, but at Barwell, as you'd expect from a leading team, there was already a wealth of knowledge and much more comprehensive telemetry interpretation expertise available to me.

The 1999 season was the expected up and down experience of a newcomer to the championship. We'd improved the diff. settings over the off-season so I was much more confident on the brakes. At Silverstone in April, we were looking good for second place before I missed just one gear shift out of Maggotts (on the International Circuit), ultimately having to settle for third. I was still not entirely happy with the high-speed balance of the car through Copse for example, where the chassis would twist at the rear and hop the car to the outside. This was particularly frustrating for me, as previously I'd always been able to make up lap time with pleasing four-wheel drifts through high-speed corners, even if most lap time gains are made in the slower-speed more technical sections. The chassis instability problem was only just manageable, but by mid-season we had improved matters, allowing Jason, James and I to enjoy a 'who can go quickest' challenge at Thruxton's super-fast Church corner, similar to the Villeneuve versus Zonta 'big balls' contest at Spa's Eau Rouge-Radillon that same year. In our case, the benchmark was 126mph minimum speed through Church with its notorious apex bump unsettling the car. Annoyingly, this exercise hardly benefitted my lap time: with a tail wind blowing up the following flat-out Brooklands section, we quickly hit the rev limiter in 6th gear as we exited the corner!

In July at Snetterton, the Vectra challenge gave me my first introduction to night racing, the exhilaration of high-speed duels in the darkness developing into an addiction that eventually drew me to the 24 hour racing I still enjoy today. I can say however that the Vectra's standard headlights were barely up to the job, the relatively flat apex kerbs being almost invisible, forcing us to drive some sections almost by memory.

Over the season, we suffered three DNFs with a tyre failure, suspension damage and the already-mentioned race-ending Morrison impact at Donington. Despite two more podium finishes at Croft and Brands Hatch, these were not enough for a top three championship position at the end of my first Vectra season. Events were also confounded by Vauxhall's bizarre decision to run a gas-powered promotional car in our races, causing mayhem as it clearly could develop as much power as they wished to give it, 'winning' several races and frequently interfering with the rest of the championship field along the way. Vauxhall eventually stuck a far bigger spanner in the works: they announced in August that the Vectra Challenge would be discontinued at end of the season! This cut short the Vectra chapter of my career, scuppering my plans to contest the championship for a second year and also putting into question the deals I'd put in place with my sponsors.

I had no choice but to look elsewhere, and thankfully found Lotus were setting up their Autobytel-sponsored one-make Sport Elise Championship within the TOCA Tour package. Lotus had the great idea to bring sponsors to each car themselves, meaning the drivers only had to find around half the budget. That worked for me as I could continue the Dexter Corporation deal (especially because the Lotus's composite body production process was somewhat relevant to their business). The Lotus sponsor assigned to my car was Anadin Ultra and yes, the season turned out to be quite a headache!

These cars with their central driving position were quite different to anything I'd driven before: a 200bhp mid-engine rear-wheel-drive package weighing less than a tonne, with quite a pitch-sensitive aero-package generating a reasonable amount of downforce. Switching from many seasons of front-wheel-drive saloon cars felt like that uncertain moment a trapeze artist lets go of one swing, before catching another. The level of the drivers around me was high, with several already having extensive single-seater experience. Adam Wilcox, who eventually won the Lotus Championship that year, had previously competed in British F3, Formula Palmer Audi and the Formula Opel Euroseries.

Pre-season, I took the opportunity to rent a road-going Elise and pound around an airfield for a day, to get a sense of how the chassis handled. As with the first time in any car, it was a matter of understanding how the Elise communicated what it was doing, a little like learning a new dialect of a language you already mostly know. You have to explore the dialect thoroughly before you can say you are fluent, and I certainly did that. Of course, that car was not running on slicks but before returning it, I may have had to draw tyre treads back onto the tyres with a black marker pen!

I then felt reasonably confident heading into the pre-season Lotus test day in Hethel. Adam was predictably quicker than me on the high-speed North Circuit there, but the tables were turned on the more twisty South Circuit, maybe marking me out as a threat to his title hopes. In the end, he need not have worried: although I ran near or at the front on many occasions, I experienced a demoralising 9 DNFs from 14 races. Only one of those was down to my error: with almost all of my experience at the time limited to relatively standard-bodied saloon cars, I had underestimated the downforce loss in the Elise when following closely. I ran wide in the leading pack, heavily impacting the tyre wall at Westfield Bend in our first race at Brands Hatch GP circuit. This was a bad weekend: I had already shunted the car in qualifying whilst avoiding a spinning Paula Cook at the old Dingle Dell. As for the rest of those DNFs, you may be surprised at some of the reasons and details shared in the 9am Dirty Tricks chapter and the 10am Keeping The Faith chapter.

In principle, there were some great things about the Lotus Championship. To offer a level playing field, the cars were all prepared by the Lotus factory team, overseen by famous names like Chris Dinnage (a mechanic on the Formula 1 cars of Ayrton Senna, Nelson Piquet, Johnny Herbert and Mike Häkkinen at Team Lotus) and vehicle dynamics guru Myles Lubbock (also of Team Lotus and Footwork Arrows fame). We also enjoyed driver coaching from ex-Formula 1 driver Martin Donnelly and met some interesting guest celebrity racers including the still very quick Tiff Needell and Boyzone singer-turned-racer Shane Lynch. I first met Shane in the race truck as we were getting changed for the Donington round. Embarrassingly, I'd forgotten Kim had painted my toe nails bright red for a laugh when I was asleep a few days before, but he didn't bat an eyelid: I guess in his popstar world, not much surprises!

A further attraction of the Lotus Championship for me was another night race at Snetterton, but even more so were the non-championship rounds at Magny Cours, a soaking-wet Spa-Francorchamps and the Nürburgring GP circuits, these being my first overseas racing opportunities. For the last, we may not have been racing in the real Green Hell, but we could all sense the menacing presence of the Nordschleife, hidden amongst the forests and peaks of the Eifel. At the time, I never realised we were driving into the track along part of its smaller relative, the old Südschleife. This was abandoned after

1971 but still mostly used as public roads down to Müllenbach. I didn't have a particularly enjoyable race on the Grand Prix track there. In qualifying I found the car was understeering excessively, a problem which we traced to poor fitment of the front 'clamshell' bodywork affecting the downforce in that area. A few spacers corrected the problem and transformed the handling, but this was all for nothing. In the race, Paula Cook (again!) destroyed the rear of my car, under braking into the Ford Kurve. Fantastically, she claimed afterwards that I had braked in what she described as a flat-out section of the track! I defy anyone in any car to go through the Ford Kurve flat out...

It would be three more years before I succumbed to the lure of the Green Hell, but not before I got my five-year plan back on track. I had stayed in touch with Barwell Motorsport, who were planning to run two Honda Accords in the 2001 BTCC season, and over the winter I began to assemble the necessary sponsor partnerships to rekindle the touring car dream.

REVERSE PERSPECTIVE

In general, the closer you get to something, the larger it appears to be. Unfortunately for me, BTCC defied this perspective, going through something of a downgrading process in the early 2000s. First, the super-successful but super-expensive 'Super-Tourers' were gone, replaced by the cost-cutting BTC Touring regulations for 2001. Running alongside this much less inspirational Touring class was a Super Production category, even more limited in terms of permitted modifications to the standard manufactured vehicle, with smaller wheels and tyres and approximately 50bhp less power. With my budget constraints, Super Production was to be my BTCC entry point, a stage where I could hopefully establish an opportunity with a Touring class works team.

Pre-season, things went well: I managed to secure around one-third of the funds I needed from Dow Automotive, largely due to the fact the BTCC offered a much higher level of TV coverage than the support championships, with two races (a sprint race and a longer 'Grand Finale' feature race) at each of the thirteen events. Curiously, the Super Production cars were not obliged to make pit stops in the feature race, unlike the Touring class, bringing about the intriguing possibility of a Super Production win.

I expected that I would be able to bring with me from Lotus funding from Dow, Anadin and Dexter, as they had always had a great time at the races and appreciated all the attention I gave them as lead sponsors of my car. As Chip Ganassi recently said, "You start expecting things in racing, you're going to be sadly disappointed." I'd hired a 'professional' to help represent me (fortunately on a 'no win, no fee' basis), but as it turned out, I could have done a better job myself. As the season approached, Anadin was poached by another BTCC team and Dexter was bought by Henkel, a competitor to Dow and a McLaren Formula 1 partner, who maybe also thought BTCC was way beneath them. This meant I'd start the season on the back foot, desperately searching for further backing, supported as far as possible by Chris Needell, Barwell's commercial director. In February, the ever-supportive Kim and I got married, Chris providing hilarious and justifiably embarrassing entertainment as my best man (his German accent is priceless!).

A couple of months later, we were on track for the first BTCC round at Brands Hatch. On the timesheets at the pre-season test, the Barwell Honda Accords had sandwiched the Peugeot 306 GTis of Simon Harrison and Roger Moen, while Gavin Pyper's Alfa Romeo 156 had also looked very quick. My Honda team mate was the highly-experienced James Kaye who had successfully campaigned the Barwell Accord over the previous season. James was not much of a talker, a Yorkshireman who kept his cards close to his chest, but within the team I could still absorb a lot about how to get the most out of the car, even if I didn't put it all together in qualifying that first race weekend at Brands Hatch.

Starting mid-pack amongst 23 cars, the sprint race went from bad to worse as I was hit at Graham Hill bend by an ambitious Matt Kelly, who the previous year had finished second in the National Saloon Cup to another BTCC Super Production rival, Toni Ruokonen. The black-and-orange flag meant I endured various visits to the pit lane to secure the flapping bumper on my way to a lowly ninth-place finish. The feature race was only slightly better, my progress delayed by a titanic back-and-forth battle for seventh with Ruokonen's Mitsubishi Carisma, that eventually fell my way.

Thruxton was much better and felt like the start of the season for me, with a sixth-place qualifying spot to James's third. I've always been a good starter, maybe carried over from my speed-skating days: by the time we all piled through Church on the first lap of the sprint race I was up to second behind Harrison. His team mate Moen attempted to restore his position, diving up the inside with our cars side by side as we rounded the first right-hand part of the Club chicane. As we then both turned left, there was no room for both our cars and Roger had to take to the grass, re-joining as I turned through the final right hander, the Accord riding up over the side of his Peugeot, with my front right wheel on his roof, eventually coming down via his windscreen and bonnet. My antics were described by TV commentator Charlie Cox as "like a rutting stag!" After getting badly blocked by the incident, James's third-place finish showed his class in the sister Honda.

Thankfully the 30-lap feature race was a smoother affair: James and I took a perfect one-two finish, setting the two fastest race laps and managing the inevitable front tyre wear which is typical of a long race at Thruxton. There was an inevitable bit of driver radio communication questioning each other's speed, but Mark rightly shut down any option of a team mate battle and we came home well ahead of Mat Jackson's Ford Focus.

By the time we got to Oulton Park in May, things were getting desperate with my funding. After differential problems in qualifying (changed by the amazing Barwell crew before the sprint race), it was a rough race to sixth. This was nothing compared to the destruction in the feature race. Another good start meant I was running fourth until my nemesis Moen took a lunge at the Knickerbrook chicane which dropped us both back. Lost momentum meant Mat Jackson saw an opportunity up the hill and into the super-fast Druids double apex right, stoving in the doors and firing me off into a huge grassy slide, a hair's breadth from the barriers. Recovering positions over the many laps remaining, I eventually passed Tom Boardman's Peugeot for fourth place in the first section of Cascades, only to be punted into a spin as Boardman used our car as a brake (for which he was penalised). Finishing eighth with all that damage was no reward for all our hard work, and Mark's fury in the paddock afterwards was a mirror of my own emotions.

I should not have been surprised the following week to receive a phone call from Chris, to explain that with the cost of all the repairs, coupled with the lack of further sponsorship on the horizon, I would have to stand down from driving duties for the foreseeable future. At Silverstone, the pain of watching substitute Simon Graves drive 'my car' (complete with Dow decals) to eighth place in the sprint race was intense. To rub salt into the wound, Simon's engine blew in the feature race, and after reviewing the telemetry, Barwell concluded I was responsible for the damage, billing me for a £10,000 engine rebuild. Should I have refused to pay, compromising our relationship and any chance of driving again that season? That's of course something I wrestled with, but the motorsport community is a small world and I wanted to preserve any reputation and trust for future seasons.

2001 still had a final sting in its tail: on the way to the TOCA end-of-season party at Brands Hatch, I lost control of my cherished BMW 325i company car when we aquaplaned across a massive flood just around a corner on the A20. Thankfully Kim and I were fine but the car wasn't, laying on its side as a write-off in the ditch, whilst we spent the evening with the locals in the pub across the road.

Early in 2002, Barwell asked if they could have my race overalls back; that felt like another slap in the face. It turned out they needed them for Tom Chilton, who they had signed to race their new BTCC Vauxhall Astra and his overalls weren't ready. At the first race, Tom stood on the podium with my name clearly visible on his belt. I'm pretty sure some folks were thinking, "What the heck happened to Pete's hair?!"

At least my experience driving Barwell's Honda Accord paid off a few weeks later, when Team B&Q Jet York City, owned by the late and totally eccentric John Batchelor, offered me a role of Test &

Development Driver. They too were running a brace of Honda Accords. John would drive a 1999 specification car, brought to the team by the other driver (we'll call him 'Junior' as he was usually accompanied by his father), who would drive the team's state-of-the-art 2001 specification car.

Initially, my role was to provide advice on set-up and help entertain the 'B&Qsi', the very enthusiastic group of fans who came to support us at each event. As it turned out, I was quickly promoted. In April, spectators at Hilltop for BTCC Round 3 at Oulton Park witnessed John have a massive accident. Subsequently, he asked me to jump into that 1999 car as reserve driver for the following races. This was a golden opportunity to recapture my BTCC dream, but it quickly developed into a nightmare.

On the face of it, things looked good at Thruxton, where, after fixing an understeer issue in qualifying, I was able to lead the sprint race until Mark Fullalove's Peugeot slammed into the side of our car, damaging the steering. Junior's father decided to remind me after the race that I should be more careful with 'their' car, just to let me know where I stood. Nevertheless, in the feature race I led the pack for a second time, until an oil leak sprayed onto my rear tyres through Noble, sending me off backwards at high speed in the approximate direction of Andover! However, we'd shown as a team we could be competitive, and Silverstone beckoned.

There, my car was down on power in qualifying, apparently due to a cracked exhaust manifold, but the sprint race thankfully threw us a curved ball weather-wise. Despite the wet track, I could see it was brightening to the southwest, so after the out lap I dived into the pit lane for slicks, along with Touring class drivers Yvan Muller, Anthony Reid and James Thomson. You would have expected carnage in such conditions; all I had to do was tip-toe through puddles, awaiting the inevitable safety car. Frustratingly, it never appeared! Everyone behaved themselves and I could only catch and pass the last few wet-tyre runners as the chequered flag was waved. Fastest lap by around five seconds wasn't much consolation either.

The feature race was more typical, and when several cars tangled at Luffield, I could move up to third until 'team mate' Junior hit me at Copse in a kind of Hamilton versus Verstappen 2021 move, bending the steering again and depriving me of second gear. At Abbey hairpin, the back of the car then took a big impact from Mark Thomas's similar Accord who eventually got past, only to fall back as it began to rain. I put a move on him into the left-hander at Priory and although we were side-by-side, Mark turned in and we both spun, Mark into the gravel whereas I could fortunately continue. Afterwards, some thug involved with Mark's team physically accosted me between the race trucks in the paddock, reminding me that the professional veneer of some BTCC teams was only skin deep.

In June, Ireland's fabulous Mondello was next up, a first visit for me at what is a genius race track, full of blind brows and off-camber corners. Designed in 1966 by racer Stuart Cosgrave, every corner has a secret and talking with the locals that week, they all had different opinions about how to tackle each one! After a wet qualifying, race day was dry. In the sprint, I managed to jump the Accord up from fourth on the grid to second around the outside at the Honda hairpin (of course!). A slow-starting Touring class car at the next left-hander blocked me from having a go at class-leading Norman Simon's BMW 320i (the German later spinning out) but in any case, a brake failure soon curtailed my race. I just about made it around Tarzan corner and infuriatingly had to retire the car in the pits.

In the feature race I finished third and Junior took second for a team double-podium. I had to endure several fraught final few laps as my electronic dashboard display had winked out and although I had big pressure from behind, I didn't want to make a risky move on my team mate lapping slightly slower ahead. Despite the great collective result and celebration afterwards, I was asked to leave the team the following week, the team manager Stuart fabricating a pretext I was obliged to accept at that time. For what it's worth, the team never saw the podium again that season. Junior's next results were 7th & 4th (Croft), 10th & DNF (Snetterton), Disqualified & 6th (Knockhill), 10th & 5th (Brands Hatch Indy), 7th & 5th (Donington).

Now that I've dragged you through my recollections of this catastrophic 2002 season, you may also like to draw your own further conclusions after reading the 9am chapter: Dirty Tricks. Despite our reasonable results, the politics, endless mechanical failures and deteriorating atmosphere in the team caused me to question why I was even racing at all. The only aspect I can say I truly enjoyed was when the door closed, the red lights went out, and all I had to deal with was the car, the track and the competition.

IT'S ABOUT TIME

Like my dad before me, I have always been one to collect and file detailed information, whether physically or mentally. It's one reason why I'm confident in writing this book, as I have so much evidential information squirrelled away from every racing season. I'm sure folks imagine they can remember quite well how things were 20 or 30 years ago. Well, I must admit in researching this book, several of my own memories had faded and needed to be corrected after diving back into those old records.

Not that my original motivation for all those notes was to write a book! At the time, it was to make sure I picked up every loose end, every clue, every detail and data point which could bring performance and podium success. I put this down to a continual feeling that, to compensate for my somewhat unorthodox and late arrival to professional racing, I needed to work harder off the track than my competitors to achieve those lap times.

Wherever we are, whatever we do, time dominates our lives. We cannot control it, at least not yet. As J.R.R. Tolkien's Gandalf so wisely said, "All we have to decide is what to do with the time that is given us." And in general, a racing driver will attempt to do more, to drive further than anyone else with the time given.

Most of us pass through this world with a perception of time measured in hours and minutes. These are ideal units of measurement to avoid missing trains, turning up late for meetings and so on. Sensibly, we use miles or kilometres 'per hour' as our definition of vehicle speed.

Occasionally, we might slice up our time into seconds, on the microwave for example, but to perceive our world in tenths, hundredths or even thousandths of a second would seem excessive and unnecessary. Yet for the racing driver, such minutia are the very essence of every working day and the difference between a flourishing career or a faded memory.

Time is the only constant in the world of every racing driver. Everything else is a variable, subject to every illusion drivers can conjure to explain their (lack of) performance. We are only as quick as the car we steer, and the only illusion time affords us is that it is always possible to drive the car faster!

Oddly, behind the wheel of a race car, time actually seems to slow as our brains become accustomed to the challenge and apparently run at a higher processing rate, creating a sensation of slow-motion that is interesting to dissect. Any road driver will have experienced how, after travelling along a high-speed motorway for an hour or two, the speed-restricted roads through a town for example seem frustratingly slow. Your brain adapted to process information on the motorway at more than double the speed and now in the town, you are going so slowly, you seem to have all the time in the world (which is a good thing for those pedestrians, cyclists or where I live, suicidal pheasants).

This slow-motion impression, the so-called Zeitraffer phenomenon, is perhaps part of our 'fight or flight' response, allowing us to deal rapidly with the intensity of high-risk conflict, including on the race track. One of many relevant examples I recall is racing ex-BTCC and Le Mans driver Eugene O'Brien at Oulton Park in a Fun Cup car (and they really are fun by the way, with great camaraderie in the paddock). We were side-by-side on the run from Hilltop down to the Hislops chicane, Eugene on my left. It was late in the day and the sun was shining out of the west. I could see his gloved hands on the wheel and every detail of his face as he turned his head slightly to check my position. We were inches apart and probably doing around 100mph at the time, yet within our respective cockpits, it may as well have been walking pace.

The first time I arrive at a new circuit, or drive a new race car, there is always an expectation of competitiveness which is tempered by my lack of experience with that particular car or venue. These days, the prediction of a racing car's lap time can be computed with incredible detail, but not so long ago, it was more down to gut-feel, based largely on engine power, car weight and tyres. Even aerodynamics was something of a black art: the famous adage 'if it looks fast, it is fast' was not always the case (as many a young rip has found, when fitting that oversized rear spoiler to their hot hatchback, resulting in nothing more than significantly worse fuel economy!).

They may not like to admit it, but the first time out of the pit lane at full throttle in a new car can be intimidating even for experienced racers, especially with high-power categories. It's a little like a ten-year-old climbing onto an adult bike: at first, everything feels slightly unstable and a little too fast. You can feel 'behind' the car for a lap or two, especially if the suspension or tyres are not working as they should. It's critical to give a driver time to acclimatise to the car and the track conditions, to build up to a complete understanding before worrying about telemetry deltas or throwing set-up changes into the mix. That luxury of time is usually not available: if a driver is given an opportunity to step up to a higher category, there is an immediate pressure to perform, to convince the team you are the right choice for the seat, even to establish yourself as the number one amongst your potential team mates. For example, I can still recall the first Vauxhall Vectra Sri V6 Challenge test at Oulton, which resulted in the two off-track excursions already described. I didn't take enough time to build up knowledge and feeling for that car and despite its challenges, especially under braking, I went too hard too soon, keen to make an impression. I was fortunate to be with an experienced and supportive team in Barwell Motorsport.

Under normal circumstances, as experience builds after a few laps, my right foot is usually trying to make a dent in the floor under the throttle pedal as my brain becomes accustomed to the speed and handling. I'm feeling 'ahead' of the car, I'm anticipating rather than reacting and as a result, I feel confident, in control and able to push. Then I come into the pits after a five-lap run and see I am a whole second off the pace. This is time playing its first trick!

Sometimes it takes a little longer to get close to the limit, depending on circumstances. An extreme example was in October 2009, when I had the incredible opportunity to test with the Aston Martin factory at the Nürburgring. Almost all of my racing to that point had been in front-wheel-drive cars. I'd raced the Nürburgring 24 hours every year since 2003 but this meant re-learning the track in a rear-wheel-drive Aston Martin V8 Vantage, with the Aston Martin Chief Instructor Wolfgang Schubauer assessing my performance from the passenger seat. As if the Nordschleife was not challenging enough, on that October morning we endured freezing temperatures, horizontal rain and a line of oil around half the track. The fine balance of going 'fast but not too fast' was the key to gaining Herr Schubauer's approval. If I was initially somewhat cautious that day, it proved to be the correct approach given the conditions and, as you'll read later, what was at stake.

Around any race track, even in perfect conditions, there are fundamental limits constraining the speed of any racing car. Anticipating that limit, staying closer to it, efficiently rescuing the car when exceeding it, exploring how it changes over the duration of a drive... these are the key skills of a winner. Simply put, it's all about the corners. As has been said by many, "Anyone can drive fast in a straight line," even if the internet is full of videos that disprove even this! A corner before or after the straight separates the racers from the wannabes.

Basic as it sounds, let's start with the corner before a relatively long straight. To be competitive, it's critical to emerge out of that corner with the highest speed possible, to maximise speed (or minimise time) along the following straight. I'll talk later about how to do that (or how not to!) but I guarantee a short race on a J-shaped track would already reveal the drivers with a more refined control of throttle and steering to maximise their corner exit and terminal speed. Adding a corner at the end of the straight would of course elevate those who also have the ability to decelerate and rotate the car at the ideal moment.

Both disciplines require a level of visualisation which is born out of experience, to know what this particular car, on this track, with these conditions, is able to do. And as mentioned earlier, experience is lacking with a new car, and sometimes visualisation is unhelpfully carried over from another car driven previously at the same circuit. We have to 'wipe' that memory file and be prepared to humbly re-learn the limits of this new car and track combination. This learning shouldn't be rushed and experimentation laps with different lines should be tagged on the telemetry for later analysis with the engineers.

The process of exploring the limits of a new car is different for different drivers. Some seem to find their limit in just a few laps, whilst others take longer but may ultimately be quicker. Some seem quick on certain corners but eternally uncompetitive on other parts of the track. A talented team mate is like gold dust in this respect, as it's then possible to review each other's telemetry and work together to combine each driver's techniques into a perfect lap.

I'll argue it is always worth taking time on each section of the track, ignoring overall lap time until each section has been maximised. To be clear, a section does not mean a single corner, but the preceding and following parts of the track which are limited by that corner. In the 1990s, when on-board telemetry was introduced, as drivers we could begin to see from the dashboard display whether we were ahead or behind the benchmark lap time at any point on the track and why. A super-late braking manoeuvre would show as a short-lived advantage, only for this to dwindle and eventually become a disadvantage along the following straight. The old Sear corner leading onto the critical Revett Straight at Snetterton was a case in point. In the Fiesta, we explored what showed on the display as faster lines behind the super-aggressive 'cow pat' apex kerbs, or running wide at the exit onto the bumpy strip of additional tarmac well beyond what today would be considered track limits. Regardless, we usually didn't arrive at the Esses any sooner!

Even then, the available telemetry was not limited to a simplistic lap time prediction. Back in the pit lane, with a skilled engineer if you were lucky enough to be driving for a top team, a far more detailed analysis could be completed, including speed, engine revs, braking points, steering inputs, g-forces, tyre temperatures and pressures. The pinnacle of this approach can be seen in the Formula 1 de-brief sessions, where the track team simultaneously scrutinises the data with the folks back at the factory. On-board cameras and computers are watching every metre of the track and as a driver, there is nowhere to hide!

An amusing aside to this occurred during a team debrief session, reviewing a playback of my driving on a cockpit camera in 2011. My team mates were in hysterics because I was feeding the steering wheel at each corner like a good candidate for a driving test! I never realised this was my steering technique, having done it subconsciously for so long. As one of my team colleagues said, "Don't stop doing it, it seems to work!" That was true at least until we progressed to the modern 'quick rack' low-ratio steering systems with fixed hand positions, which initially gave me horrible hand-cramps!

Back at Barwell, my telemetry fascination meant I developed something of a reputation as a 'data-junkie'. The team all had nicknames and thanks to my Dexter-yellow race-suit, I was 'Cato', a name that's pretty much stuck ever since, other than a brief period where 'Dato' was unsuccessfully tried as an alternative! With fast team mates, the temptation to compare every lost micro-second in the telemetry is strong, testing the patience of even the most willing engineer, still in the race truck at 10pm. I can only say, in my case this effort was rewarded with quantifiable lap time improvements, the data analysis providing me with accelerated guidance for adapting driving styles or lines. It's those critical tenths and hundredths that elevate a car from the mine-field of the mid-field to front of the grid glory!

TELL IT LIKE IT IS

Developing a close and trusting relationship with team engineers is a key component of success. That means being able to describe the car's behaviour confidently and effectively, most specifically in areas of the track where lap time is lost, information which can then be acted upon in terms of set-up adjustments or even fault finding. It's not enough to complain, "The car's crap!" as I heard from a reliable source was one well-known Formula 1 driver's testing feedback, before handing the car over to the test driver.

I spent a lot of time in the pit garage, establishing credibility with the engineers and mechanics by demonstrating understanding of the hardware I was piloting. Credibility is important: I've always relied heavily on my further education in mechanical engineering, taking time to appreciate how the car is built, how its systems work and what element of this could be responsible for a particular response out on track. With that knowledge programmed in, I could store information around the lap, relaying it back to the engineers in the debrief in that 'slow-motion' format described earlier, providing them with bite-sized actionable chunks. It may take well over a minute to properly describe the intricacies of how the race car is responding on a piece of track which takes five seconds to drive in reality!

This super-detailed approach is even more important today, as modern race cars have become ever more complex. Electronic driver aids are supplementing the basic mechanical package, that in some ways reduce the driving challenge (not to mention the number of pedals), but add to the sensations we need to pick up on as drivers if we are to differentiate ourselves. Back at Team Touraco in the late 1980s, I recall a guy pounding around in a Mercedes 190 Cosworth equipped with an early ABS. He'd mash the brake every lap and we could hear it chatter as it slewed into the Cadwell Park short circuit hairpin. He parked it all ticking and hot, and then on his first lap after lunch, he speared straight on into the tyres at the base of the Mountain. The ABS had cooked itself and the driver had lost all feeling for the brakes, having become totally reliant on the electronic assistance. Nowadays, such systems are commonplace and super-reliable. In a modern GT3, a competent amateur driver is able to lap relatively close to a professional driver's pace, thanks largely to the prior thousands of hours of vehicle dynamics and handling development, advancing the braking and stability control systems which prevent excessive loss of front or rear grip.

In 2017, I drove the awesome Aston Martin Racing's GT3 at the Nürburgring. I was amazed at how predictable and stable it was compared to lesser versions of the Vantage. Braking in the GT3 involved mashing the pedal as hard as possible; we are talking around 120 bar pressure in comparison to the 70 bar I initially thought to be appropriate. The race ABS system kicked in as the speed and aerodynamic downforce decreased into the corner, rotating the car all the way to the apex with almost no trace of understeer or oversteer. The paddle-shift gear box meant there was no use of a clutch pedal (other than for pit stop halts), eliminating any need for foot sensitivity during gear changes. From the apex on, the throttle could be applied with aggression, the traction control dealing with any potential tyre slip.

Of course, I'm simplifying the process. To be quick in a GT3 requires an even finer understanding of these systems to get the most out of the car, especially over a race distance as fuel load and tyre grip are reduced. The margins between competitors at that level are miniscule, and amateur drivers who rely too much on those driver aids will never achieve a position at the front of the grid. That day I was happy to still be able to turn in respectable lap times, on par with those set by GT3 expert Jonny Adam who was kind enough to advise me. A trusted team mate like Jonny is critical. There will always be those drivers who blithely tell you "Oh yes, I'm flat through there!" or, "I brake at 50 meters into that one." All the more reason to get into their telemetry. In general though, another driver will be able to tell you how to extract the most out of the car more effectively than an engineer can.

Working with Mark Lemmer at Barwell for example brought the advantage of a team principle who was also a very competent racer. He could advise to a level I'd never experienced up to that point, even by observing trackside. I remember at Snetterton, Mark advised I changed my line at the chicane with the Vectra to what felt like an overly-aggressive entry which completely transformed the exit and speed up the following straight. Even today, I'm always open to trying new techniques if it brings lap time benefits.

Certainly, too much pit wall interference with driving style can result in disaster. As a recent example, at the 2023 Monaco Grand Prix, the Alpha Tauri pit instructed Yuki Tsunoda to alter his braking as the rain fell in the latter stages of the race. His radio response was classic Yuki: "Are you trying to crash me?!" A few laps later he went straight on under braking at Mirabeau (or Turn 5 as they call it). Knowledgeable folks on the pit wall can advise, but the driver in the car at that moment should make the final call, as I learned with my race-ending crash at Kesselchen in 2016 Nürburgring 24 hours race.

That year, the Aston Martin factory team were fielding the lighter-weight GT8 which proved a very effective SP8 class weapon on the twists and turns of the Nordschleife, the #42 car emerging into a damp dawn with a healthy class lead of more than two laps. With conditions threatening rain, I took over mid-morning for another double stint, the first on intermediate tyres, the second on slicks after a brief radio discussion, as the team's weather radar showed the rain which had started to fall was to be short-lived. In fact, it was that second stint that proved to be short-lived. On the first lap out of the pits, with just four hours left in the race, I came up behind a BMW back-marker, who considerately moved left approaching the sixth gear Kesselchen corner. To make sure I didn't tag the BMW, I put the car a tyre's width to the right of the apex kerb, just off the drier line, and the slicks simply let go, pitching the car heavily into the barrier. Game over. With the massive class lead we had, I should have insisted upon intermediate tyres, even if it meant lost time for a further pit stop. I had seen the track conditions. I should have overruled the pit call for slicks and of course I should have waited to pass that BMW on the following straight.

Certainly, there are much less obvious instances where a driver's feedback is critical to identify the problem before it becomes a major issue. An example next up on the scale of obviousness is a damper failure, that can be characterised in different ways depending upon the specific malfunction, but in general resulting in less control of the spring on that corner of car and reduced handling control as a result. Unfortunately, dampers don't necessarily have to fail to still be a problem: on several occasions, I've experienced sealed dampers in highly-professional categories where one performs quite differently to another as a result of manufacturing and assembly tolerances. It becomes important to match pairs of dampers in such circumstances.

In addition to having a fundamental understanding of how the various suspension systems work, it requires a great deal of sensitivity and confidence to pick up these nuances on track. A recent example I can share was a handling issue which became evident in the 2021 Nürburgring 24 hours race. I was behind the wheel of a Porsche 718 Cayman GTS in the SP4-T class. The race was split into two halves by a red flag due to dense fog. In those last few laps before the stoppage, I had a slight sensation, only in left-handers, that the car was steering at the right rear (or 'loose' as our American friends like to say). It was almost a helpful attribute as the car was predominantly limited by understeer (more so than I would have liked), a set-up intended to be comfortable for all four drivers sharing that car. Nevertheless, I radioed in quite specific details about these symptoms (I tend to over-communicate in the car: the Nordschleife is a long lap and it can get pretty lonely!). As we were called into the pits by the red flag, the Köppen team set about investigating. Nothing seemed amiss until they found a control arm bushing which was slightly loose, that being enough to alter the dynamics of the suspension movement. As the cars were not under *parc fermé* rules, we changed the component and when I took the restart, the car was immediately stable and symmetrical at the rear. Had we not identified the issue, perhaps that bushing would have failed mid-race with serious consequences, or at the very least cost us what became another class win that year.

More recently, driving a different Porsche Cayman, this time in the hotly-contested Porsche Endurance Trophy Nürburgring Cup 3 class with Mathol Racing, we suffered some hellish few days of qualifying. At the Nürburgring 24 hours race from Thursday to Saturday morning, there are three qualifying sessions and a warm-up. Right from the first session, all the team's drivers could feel an instability under braking, a twisting sensation which excessively activated the ABS and ESC systems. Despite a lap time good enough for P5 in class, we were sure there was something amiss. Thanks to a solid driver relationship with the team's engineers and mechanics, we could convince them over the next days to complete a marathon replacement of dampers, springs, anti-roll bar, drive shafts and all relevant electronics sensors, with the kind assistance from Porsche Motorsport. Incredibly, just a few minutes before the race start, a strut brace bolt located out of sight behind the left front shock tower was found to be loose. With no time remaining, we took the start and at each scheduled pit stop, we made the necessary adjustment to recover the set-up, something we never fully achieved. It was only during the strip-down after the race that the team also found the rear sub-frame to be slightly bent. These mechanical issues caused a handling asymmetry which was enough to fool the electronics and trigger all sorts of unhelpful responses. This is not a criticism of the team: it simply highlights that even with all the sophistication of modern race cars, the fundamentals are still critical.

Interestingly, in that race, had one of my team mates not been hit with a penalty for a flag infringement in qualifying, we would not have incurred a pit lane start and two-minute penalty. We would have had to go to the grid for the formation lap an hour before we found the problem with the strut brace. As is so often the case in motorsport, the lows can rapidly turn into highs: with nothing to lose, we drove that Cayman for 24 hours at what felt like the limit, the team being rewarded the next afternoon with a hard-fought second place. The Cup 3 class is hotly contested by many up-and-coming young drivers, so this was a particularly satisfying result for me, proving age is no barrier at the Green Hell. Perhaps it even lends some useful authority during debates with younger team mates and engineers in debrief sessions!

Nevertheless, in 2022, my first time racing with Mathol, I did not use all my years of experience to good effect. We had a great start in Cup 3, up to P3 from P7 on the grid. In my second stint, driving into dusk, I hit oil under braking from 170mph (274kmh) at Tiergarten, just managing to keep it out of the barrier after an armful of opposite lock over the grass and gravel on the left. After such a frantic moment,

I should have radioed the team, but as I was already past the pit entry, I decided to drive the GP track to assess if there was any damage. At first the car was all over the place but as the tyres cleaned up, it felt pretty normal. I was in two minds whether to play it safe and dive into the pits via the 'back door' for a quick check, or continue out onto the Nordschleife. Competitiveness got the better of me and I was punished with a front-left puncture just a few kilometres later on the descent through Hatzenbach. This cost us around 20 minutes as I crawled around the whole lap back to the pits, dodging cars streaking by. If I had trusted my instincts and gone in for the quick check, we probably would have lost less than five minutes.

In that moment, I lost sight of the bigger picture: a radio call to the team would most likely have resulted in a different outcome. In the end, it was of no consequence, because the car was terminally crashed at Schwedenkreuz by a team mate (who was thankfully unharmed). Nevertheless, the learning is clear: if in doubt, be honest and involve the team. Even if nothing else, you'll be able to share the blame when it goes wrong, which at some point, it inevitably will!

THE LIMIT

The 'limit' is probably one of the most over-used expressions in the paddock. It's a term frequently used, especially by drivers, to describe the maximum possible speed of the car through a particular section of track, a lap or even a race distance. Despite the desire of fans to elevate their heroes' achievements, even the world's most successful drivers' claims that they drove to the limit by 'extracting the maximum' from the car, is most certainly false! Owing to the fact that human beings are designing and controlling the race cars, there is always an element of human error, and therefore always a potential for more lap time reduction. This is why motorsport is endlessly fascinating and challenging: the limit is ever-moving, a notional extent of available performance.

I had the great fortune to share a Nürburgring 24 hours race victory in the Aston Martin GT8 with the super-talented and suitably-crazy Viking Nicki Thiim, one part of the famous 'Dane-train' who have achieved so much success together. In discussion, Nicki explained his approach was to go beyond the limit to find it, his self-belief depending upon his ability to bring the car back under control. It's a compelling idea, and one that undoubtedly works on forgiving tracks where there is physical room for error. Aside from my very early ignorant ventures onto (and off) the track, my attitude has always been slightly more cautious than Nicki's. I suspect this is why I have gone well over the two decades I've raced at the Nordschleife, an unforgiving place where exceeding the limit is not a choice, as so many have found. More of this in the 2pm Inside Track chapter, where I'll discuss track designs that in my view best represent the towering challenge motorsport should provide.

Nevertheless, let's consider this concept of a limit and what defines it. Imagine a race car driving around a smooth, circular track with a fixed radius. The car eventually reaches a speed above which it begins to lose grip, running wide and losing time. That's the limit, right? Wrong! Even in this simplest of scenarios, there are so many factors influencing that loss of grip. Ignoring at this point the optimal set-up and engineering of the car and tyres (that will be covered in the 1am It's A Set-Up chapter), we'll talk first about the dynamics of the vehicle as it approaches this perceived limit.

The car and driver stay in touch with the track via the 'contact patch' of the tyres. The contact patch of any tyre has a maximum load carrying capability, determined by friction, contact patch size and the dynamic transfer of vertical load on the tyre through the suspension. If, for example, the acceleration of the vehicle (in other words the rate of speed increase) is altered, this will change the vertical load on each tyre. Consider front-wheel-drive cars like my old Fiesta, Vectra, Honda BTCC car and others. Hard acceleration in a relatively constant radius corner like Luffield at Silverstone would transfer weight from the front to the rear tyres. Since the grip of a tyre is proportional to the vertical load applied to it (albeit not linearly proportional), the car would start to understeer as front vertical load is decreased. A quick confidence lift of the throttle would temporarily add front load and lateral grip, but now of course we are oscillating around the limit and we're losing time.

In this front-wheel-drive scenario, as the load moves rearwards, not only are we losing front lateral grip but also we're losing traction on the driven wheels which otherwise would help us rotate the car around the radius of the corner. A rear-wheel-drive car may respond similarly with regard to loss of frontal grip, the main difference being that at least the load is being added to the driven wheels, so traction should be aided. Nonetheless, it's clear we are already far from the limit in either case.

Some would counter that with a rear-wheel-drive car, it's possible to 'boot it through the corner', rotating the car with the throttle by sliding the rear. This reduces the lateral demand on the front tyres. Even if undesirable in modern Formula 1, the technique has been used for decades in classic racing, much to the enjoyment of drivers and spectators, just like the four-wheel-drifts I enjoyed in that Frogeye Sprite. Turning that car into a corner with insufficient throttle would soon reveal the limitation of front tyre grip. The only (quick) solution was to steer the Sprite by inducing rear tyre 'slip'. If it's done to perfection, there is very little oversteer evident with the steering wheel.

A certain amount of tyre slip angle (the difference between the direction of travel versus the direction of the tyre) in fact increases the coefficient of friction between tyre and track, but only up to a maximum, depending upon the tyre construction. When we allow one end of the car to slip, to a certain extent we can maximise lateral grip there, but too much slip becomes a slide as grip is lost. It's a balancing act, using the throttle to maintain optimum levels of slip angle and vertical load on each tyre. I've used this technique through all my years racing rear-wheel-drive Aston Martins and Porsches, the trick nowadays also being to minimise steering angle to avoid triggering the traction control or stability control systems that deprive us of corner exit speed.

Slip is also a factor in traction. In this case, slip refers to the difference between the vehicle speed versus the speed of tyre rotation: the greater the difference, the higher the slip. As an extreme example, as can be seen from the clouds of rubber smoke during burn outs, excessive tyre slip on acceleration will result in the contact patch losing grip. Similarly, when braking, where the tyre rotational speed is slower than the vehicle speed, excessive slip will result in a 'lock up' and a loss of friction which reduces grip and deceleration.

As with a combination of cornering and acceleration, braking whilst cornering places even more demand on those tyre contact patches. A technique known as 'trail braking' is a manipulation of weight transfer, loading the outside front tyre whilst decreasing rear grip to help rotate the car. In reality, that outside front tyre can easily become overloaded, decreasing braking capability relative to straight-line braking, but in the cut-and-thrust of real racing, such techniques are essential to permit successful overtakes. In the late

1990s, I remember watching Formula 1 maestro Michael Schumacher braking into the right-hand Copse corner at Silverstone so much later than anyone else, it almost looked like he'd overshot each time. Clearly his Ferrari could accommodate the additional load on the front left, a set-up his team mates at the time appeared to struggle with. In modern cars such as the Cup 3 Cayman, the electronic systems actually require use of trail-braking to be competitive. Modern fast-processing ECUs and actuators provide different levels of braking pressure for each wheel, helping to rotate the car towards the apex by controlling braking forces across the axles. Relatively recently, I've had to recalibrate my own braking techniques to effectively exploit these electronic driver aids.

All of the above assumes the track is smooth and consistent. In reality, clearly this is not the case: any stretch of race track will contain a unique set of features which determine the available grip level. First, at a macro-scale, the camber of the track will either add to or detract from the vertical load on the tyres, depending on whether that camber is positive (tilting the car towards the inside of the corner) or negative, sometimes called adverse (tilting the car away from the inside of the corner). A radical race track example of positive camber is the banked Caracciola Karussell corner at the Nürburgring, named after Rudolf Caracciola who, at the German 1931 Grand Prix first dipped the wheels of his Mercedes SSKL into the drainage ditch at this hairpin. Today this 'ditch' is paved with concrete and is a *bona-fide* part of the race track. As we approach, the banked section of the Karussell is in fact not visible behind a crest (leading novices to overshoot the entry), but once we drop into the banking, the mid-corner load sensation is almost more vertical than horizontal. In fact, this corner can be the limiting factor for ride height, as springs are compressed and critical components will impact the concrete if the car is run too low. More will be shared on what it's really like to drive the Karussell (and indeed the whole Nordschleife lap) in the timed on-board lap you'll experience in the 3pm One Hell Of A Lap chapter!

Other smaller-scale track surface features will also disturb the tyre contact patch and vertical load level, contributing to the total amount of available grip. Snooker-table smooth, flat circuits like Silverstone or Magny Cours enable a driver to approach the limit in a more precise way compared to rougher tracks such as the COTA (Circuit of the Americas), Sebring or of course, the Nordschleife. To be fast at these tracks requires a certain trust in the track, a belief that the temporary loss of grip will be returned as the tyre re-establishes contact with the asphalt beyond. COTA is somewhat unique in the sense that the track was built on soft ground, and as a result, subsidence had led to bumps which are unacceptable (at least by Formula 1 standards). The crests of these bumps have been mechanically ground down, with only moderate success: the track now offers varying levels of grip depending on whether the asphalt surface is original or ground. This for example meant modulating braking force or steering angle when we raced the Aston Martin Vantage GT8 there, in anticipation of the grip loss, if the 'limit' was to be approached.

An even higher level of anticipation is required all the way around the Nordschleife, where the extreme bumps, jumps and high kerbs are unnerving for the newcomer, but essential to deeply understand in pursuit of a quick lap time. After completing many hundreds of racing laps there, those features are indelibly printed into my subconscious, momentary grip losses being anticipated without need to adjust steering angle or throttle. Even so, this mountainous track can change from one season to the next, bumps receding or becoming more severe over the winter. To further the challenge, pre-season track repairs at the Green Hell often constitute only half a track-width of new asphalt, the grip level varying enormously, especially in the rain, as the tyres transition from the new to the old surface and vice versa. A slight change of line will completely change this sequence, bringing the tyres into contact with a new set of bumps, with catastrophic consequences in the worst case.

We can't talk about the Nordschleife without talking about the weather, certainly also a feature at most other tracks, but none so extreme. In a single 24 hour race there, we've driven through baking sunshine, torrential rain and floods, fog, gale force winds, hail, and one even ended with a snow-covered track, such is May in the Eifel! With a lap distance of almost 16 miles (25.378km to be exact) and 300 metres of elevation change, it's quite possible to encounter a combination of these conditions over a single lap, not to mention the presence of oil or other fluids on track. All these affect the 'limit' of any given section at that moment in time, often requiring quick driver reactions to avert disaster, although sometimes even that is not enough.

In 2016, when a violent but very localised hailstorm ravaged the Nürburgring 24 hours race, Aston Martin factory driver team mate Darren Turner was at the wheel of our GT8 approaching Schwedenkreuz, when he somehow became aware that something ahead was amiss. It was enough for him to back off a little, a move that enabled him to be the first car to survive the carnage at Aremberg. More than 20 cars crashed there and many others were comically stranded on the track, their slicks not finding any traction on the icy surface. Whatever enabled Darren to subconsciously pick up on the tiny differences that permitted him to predict the forthcoming limit change, he'll admit it's not something that can be relied upon with impunity! The limit can and will change in a matter of seconds...

Up to now, we have considered the limit in the context of uninterrupted driving on traffic-free track, an unlikely race-day scenario. I can count on one hand the number of laps at the Nordschleife where I have not either overtaken or been passed by another car, compromising my position on track and therefore changing the 'limit' at that point. In 2003, in my first race at the Green Hell, I drove it like an elongated sprint race, taking every opportunity to close up to the traffic ahead, diving left and right to find a way past. These days, with the benefit of experience, I can better anticipate where I will catch those cars ahead, using my momentum to carry me safely past with no appreciable loss of lap time. It's a technique that acknowledges the limit has to be modified in traffic, but with the right timing, the impact can be minimised. The temporary time loss from briefly remaining behind the car ahead can even be counteracted by the slipstream benefit on the following straight.

I hope by detailing at least some of the complexity in this chapter, I have explained why driving on the 'limit' is no simple matter and is never truly achieved, despite the assertions of those anxious to protect their driving careers! There are so many controlled and uncontrolled factors involved at the limit, each one influencing the other. Each track, sometimes each lap, leads to a different definition of that limit, and the stakes are high if you misjudge it.

Many have quoted Niki Lauda who supposedly said in 1984, "The secret is to win going as slowly as possible." The truth is, winners work closely with their engineers to set up their cars such that their limit is beyond that of their competitors. If the job is done well, they don't need to drive near their limit at all, much to the disappointment of observant motorsport fans in periods of single-team dominance. That's a shame for the sport and also for the drivers: there is undeniably a huge amount of satisfaction associated with driving near the limit, or recovering a car that has slightly exceeded it!

IT'S A SET-UP

In any competitive situation, a winner will constantly look to gain an edge, however insignificant or, in the case of my first year contemporaries at Coventry University, however meaningless! In our design studio, a long room of desks arranged like American city blocks, we were provided with 'wheelie-chairs' on five-spoke castors. It didn't take long for these to be re-purposed as competition vehicles, ride height fully lowered for maximum leg-extension and cornering stability; you could regularly hear the rumble of speeding chairs from outside the door! Unfortunately, our fun was curtailed when the head of the course David Browne witnessed a nasty crash into his office door, despite perpetrator Tim legging it from the scene. We had to resort to quieter competition formats, inventing 'chair chess', where the distance from a single push was far more important than cornering capability. I knew I was amongst friends when I arrived at the studio early one morning to 'tune' my chair by removing the fluff from the castors, only to find several other guys with their chairs upturned on the desks, doing precisely the same thing! All this illustrates the importance of preparation and set-up, regardless of the contested race category!

When it comes to motorsport, many don't like to acknowledge the 'elephant in the garage', which is the significantly greater importance of car set-up and preparation versus the actual driving of the car. Of course, both need to work in harmony and be executed to a high standard, but a world champion driver in a bad car will simply not be in a position to win. It's the motorsport equivalent of giving Roger Federer a smaller racquet. For example, casual fans were quick to criticise multiple Formula 1 world champion Lewis Hamilton's fall from the podium in 2022 but as those with more insight could see, it was the Mercedes-AMG Petronas Formula 1 Team that fell, not Lewis: he was literally set up to fail that season.

The same is true at all levels of motorsport, even if the interest and the hype is mainly around the drivers. For this reason, it's a good idea for anyone serious about getting behind the wheel to leave their ego at home, find the best possible car and team and be ready to work hard together with the engineers to maximise its performance. Especially in a strictly controlled category, such as the one-make Fiesta or Vectra championships I contested, regulations prevent extensive modifications and so the set-up challenge is about many minor changes which combine to bring about a hopefully significant benefit out on track.

There are three fundamental ways teams pursue this goal:

1. Optimise areas that are permitted by the championship technical regulations (a must-have capability).
2. Optimise (and usually hide) areas that are not included in the regulations (arguably the most creative activity).

3. Optimise (and definitely hide) areas that are expressly not permitted by the regulations (otherwise called cheating).

The first category is a fundamental part of being competitive, especially in those highly-controlled one-make championships where a lost tenth of a second can be disastrous. Assuming engine and gearbox are sealed, teams will focus on maximising corner speeds via optimisation of mechanical grip. Depending on championship regulations, this will include tuning of tyre pressures, ride heights (and corner-weights), springs, anti-roll bars, damper settings (high- and low-speed bump and rebound) and suspension geometry (camber, caster, toe). Added to this will be tuning of the aerodynamic package (that must also accommodate suspension movement, especially pitch) as dictated by the available wing and rake angles.

It's not my intent here to dive deeply into the science of race car set-up; there are many useful reference sources for that. Nevertheless, a driver who spends time understanding the influence of all the adjustable components on the handling of the race car will provide more accurate, efficient feedback, a useful advantage where pre-event testing sessions are time limited.

Before we even start to consider possible adjustments, it's worth pointing out the difference between preparation and set-up. Preparation is making sure everything is built and assembled perfectly, so it operates optimally. Only with this level of attention can set-up alterations be meaningful and consistent, allowing the driver to recognise how set-up changes feel, to the extent that useful feedback can be provided to the engineer. I have driven for highly professional teams where the engineer prefers the driver to simply describe the dynamic handling characteristics of the car, without attempting to diagnose the technical reasons behind any problematic behaviour. Personally, I find the collaboration works better when both driver and engineer have a good comprehension of each other's area of expertise. The driver certainly needs to have a high degree of sensitivity and experience to properly assess the influence of set-up changes. Having said that, I know of more than one occasion where the engineer has indicated a 'demon tweak' has been implemented and the driver has gone quicker, even though no change was made at all!

Like the best magic tricks, you may think you have understood how to set the car up to be as fast as possible but there is always more speed hidden, as you'll discover afterwards! This is a never-ending challenge, not least because the various components involved all interact with each other, functioning as one system, meaning all must be optimised together. To take just one simplistic example, adjustment of a front anti-roll bar will affect dynamic load transfer and therefore optimal spring and damper settings at the front, but also at the rear. Sometimes one element can dominate, such as the highly sensitive tyre pressures on the Porsche Cayman Cup 3 car which we found could destroy a set-up that worked perfectly well on a previous set of tyres with slightly different pressures. The magnitude of the set-up task becomes even more evident when we also super-impose the complexity of different tracks, changing track conditions, fuel load and tyre wear, not to mention the emergence of advanced electronic driver aids and different driving styles and abilities within the team.

Endurance racing is an unusual motorsport discipline. Unlike the sprint categories I had contested prior to 2003, endurance racing truly creates team mates (and great friends!) with a common interest in helping to make the car go quicker, sharing experiences and telemetry to achieve the best result together. In fact, successful endurance racers recognise that the car needs to be comfortable for the *slowest* of the team's drivers. If that driver gains confidence in the car, their lap time improvements will be far greater than the marginal improvements of the quickest drivers in the team. Equally, if the car is set up on a knife-edge, it may be quick but difficult to handle, especially for the less-experienced driver. In 2019, our sister #36 Aston Martin was set up by Chris Goodwin, then high-performance test driver at Aston Martin, who opted for an aggressive approach which was quick in qualifying but degraded the rear tyres over a race stint compared to the more compliant tyre-friendly solution in our #37 Vantage. Ultimately, perhaps as a result of the more nervous set-up, the least-experienced of Chris's team mates, racing journalist Christian Gebhardt, crashed the #36 heavily at the 'Miss-Hit-Miss' corner before Wehrseifen, ending their race.

My own racing career led me through a huge variety of racing cars, each built to differing regulations and each requiring a unique set-up approach to extract the maximum at any given track in any given set of conditions. Even in the early days, I made my own set-up sheets and built up a detailed knowledge of our set-up directions and their effects. This was the route to establishing a meaningful advantage over competition, especially when an engine power increase was not an affordable option.

Sometimes the ideal set-up is not initially easy to handle and requires driver adaption to extract the maximum from the package. A willingness to persevere with new approaches, even quite extreme configurations, is then a helpful attribute, even if these ideas come from outside the team. In 1997, whilst racing the Fiesta with Mark Fish Motorsport, I first came into contact with Pat Martin, then an engineer at Barwell Motorsport, who had previous experience with the NASCAR Truck Series. These were typically raced on oval tracks with a set-up to optimise the cars' balance through those long left-hand curves. Our Fiesta of course raced on tracks with both left- and right-handers, but at each track, there were certain critical corners which had a greater influence on lap time, where we were looking for an advantage, even if it meant a slight disadvantage on other less significant corners.

Brands Hatch Indy circuit was a case in point: with one exception, all the key corners were right handers. Understeer restricted our mid-corner speed through these corners, the limit set by the maximum amount of front camber allowed by the Fiesta bodyshell geometry and by the technical regulations. Pat suggested an asymmetrical NASCAR style set-up, raising the ride height on the left side to effectively achieve more camber angle on that side. Out on track, the car rode totally flat through Paddock, Druids and Clearways, dramatically helping grip. In the tent, we had to park the car with the steering wheel on full lock to disguise the tweak, which was obvious to anyone looking at the car front on. We successfully used variations of this development at the following Silverstone International double-header, the time loss through the left-handers at Priory and Brooklands being more than compensated for around the rest of the lap. A couple of years later, I was amused to see Mark Fish's Renault Clio Cup cars also parked on full lock in the paddock at Brands Hatch. Equally entertaining was then watching one of his drivers finding out the set-up didn't work so well through left-handers when he ran wide at Graham Hill Bend!

Mark and I had even tried playing with the wheelbase of the left side versus the right by altering caster settings, a bit like a Renault 4 which was built with the front left forward of the front right! All of this was totally legal, with ride height, camber and caster adjustments all allowed and scrutineered.

Where things become murky are the second category of 'adjustments' not included in championship regulations. Of course, motorsport should fundamentally allow close and fair racing, the rules preventing or at least limiting an unfair advantage if it threatens to detract from the on-track contest. The reality is that there is a similar close-fought off-track contest amongst the teams' engineers. Just like track limits, as soon as there is a rule, they will probe it for weaknesses and cross that line if they can get away with it.

For instance, there was a specific ride-height tweak we employed with the BTCC Honda Accord. A race car in general will benefit from a reduced ride height, lowering the centre of gravity and reducing body roll. This is why ride heights are frequently checked by the championship officials, using a simple roller device on a flat patch in the pit lane. The Honda had one particular low point on the chassis, a welded joint that meant the whole car had to be raised a few millimetres to compensate. It was advantageous when this tiny protrusion was ground off, on a kerb of course!

A stock race car bodyshell, being based upon a road car, is never going to provide the optimal platform for the race suspension or slick tyres. Car makers engineer their vehicles to meet crash or fuel efficiency regulations and durability or comfort requirements which have little to nothing in common with those of racing cars. Ideally a racing car body would be as stiff and as lightweight as possible, the only compliance provided by the suspension system. In this way, the dynamic load transfer (described in the 12am The Limit chapter and 1am It's A Set-Up chapter) can be most effectively controlled and tuned. Any road-car-based racing car is then a compromise, and engineers will look for methods to improve matters.

One such method was to recognise the contribution of the front windscreen (and the rear window in a saloon/sedan) to the torsional (twisting) stiffness of the bodyshell. These glass components are bonded into the bodyshell using a formulated semi-structural adhesive specified by the original car maker. The modulus of that adhesive is a parameter that describes its stiffness once cured. If the modulus is too high, the adhesive is too stiff and the windscreen may crack if, for example, the vehicle hits a pothole. For this reason, car makers tend to specify more flexible glass-bonding adhesives for road cars.

On the race track, it's unlikely the car will hit a pothole, although to be fair, some kerbs can be equally aggressive if approached incorrectly! There is a benefit to selecting non-regulated higher-modulus windscreen repair adhesives, the incentive being to increase the torsional stiffness contribution to the bodyshell. Certainly, the performance gain is not as extreme as in a road car, because the relative stiffness of a race car is of course already increased by the presence of triangulated roll-cage tubing, typically welded into the bodyshell, specifically at the suspension towers. Nevertheless, with every tenth of a second equating to multiple grid spots, any advantage was worth the bother, even when it resulted in multiple cracked windscreen replacements, as with the 1999 Vauxhall Vectra with its far-too-flexible body. That car required more than enhanced glass bonding to stabilise the bodyshell.

A further stiffness modification widely known to teams and scrutineers was to allow super glue to seep into the gaps between the existing body spot-welds, effectively creating continuous seam welds along the joint lines. Unfortunately for those trying this method, to be fully effective, it really requires paint removal to allow adhesive penetration into the joint and adhesion to the metal beneath. Furthermore, standard super glue is not ideal: it is relatively brittle and not particularly robust after exposure to hot, wet conditions. Yes indeed, I did learn a bit of adhesive chemistry from my time working with Dow Automotive!

Next to stiffness, weight is the other major area of engineering advantage and hence is closely monitored. It's common these days to see a car being called onto the weight scales directly in the pit lane, to ensure it is not underweight. Lotus founder Colin Chapman was obsessed with reducing the weight of his cars, famously stating, "Adding power makes you faster on the straights, but subtracting weight makes you faster everywhere." Any moving mass will continue in the direction it is travelling until acted upon by another force. The greater the mass, the greater the force required to alter its speed or trajectory. A race car is no different. A lower vehicle weight requires less braking force to decelerate it, reduces the demand upon the tyres to change its direction into a corner, and less power to accelerate it again on the corner exit. It is also clear that there is a virtuous circle associated with decreasing weight: a lighter car can use a smaller engine, drivetrain, brakes and suspension, thereby saving even more weight.

But how can a race team reduce car weight when the regulations specify a minimum which is frequently checked? The short answer is, they can't, but they might try to illegally move it around within the car! In most one-make race categories, we are definitely now into the third 'cheating' category of tweaks. Most race cars have an overriding pre-set weight distribution due to their base configuration that limits the handling of the car at one end or the other. For example, a front-engined car will usually understeer, because the weight at the front is higher than at the rear: assuming no mitigating suspension adjustments, the lateral weight transfer in a corner will be greater at the front, eventually exceeding the traction capability of the front tyres before the rears let go. Achieving a more balanced weight distribution, maximising the work done by all four tyres, is what the engineers target.

Back in the early less-regulated days of our Alfasud, we made crude attempts to improve the weight distribution by removing unnecessary metal, for example inside the front plastic bumper. We even removed the heavy rear spoiler to reduce overall weight, but the weight distribution penalty meant we put it back at the next race, just as several other 'Suds had amusingly removed theirs in response! TOCA Fiesta and Vectra regulations allowed no such liberties, not even permitting added ballast in strategic locations to improve balance. One rumoured and very extreme cheat was alleged to have involved a Vectra bodyshell being acid-dipped to reduce overall metal thickness. The eliminated mass was added back into the floor to helpfully move the weight distribution rearwards and also to lower the centre of gravity, helping to minimise the effects of the centrifugal forces which attempt to overturn a cornering vehicle. With the car repainted in the body shop, the weigh scales would have shown a legally acceptable total and the scrutineers would never have noticed anything was amiss!

Back on safer ground, one aspect of weight distribution in a typical stock car is the asymmetry across the car, with the driver sitting either on one side of the other. Depending on the car and driver, we could be talking about an additional 5-10% of the total car mass sitting in the racing seat! This can be compensated through proper set-up of the corner-weights (the static weight on each wheel) by adjusting the relative ride height of each spring platform such that the sum of the diagonal corner-weights is equal. One tip: when measuring this, don't trust the so-called flat-patches at the race track, as they are rarely flat and will provide misleading corner-weight readings. Done correctly, this basic set-up provides a similar 'feel' in left- and right-hand corners. Handling imbalances can then be mitigated by further individual ride height adjustments to control desired dynamic transfer weight around the car. It seemed to me that this fundamental concept wasn't properly understood by my 2002 team mate or by his BTCC crew, as evidenced by their requests for my Barwell's Honda Accord set-up information. In my opinion, their decline in results is obvious after I left the team and stopped sharing set-up guidance.

A further major influence on race car performance is, of course the amount of motive power at the wheels, despite Colin Chapman's preferences. At a simplistic level, any attempt to manipulate fuel- or air-flow into the engine or to reduce frictional losses within the engine and drive train will alter the performance of the system. In one-make racing, this has long been controlled by engine and gearbox scrutineering seals which cannot be tampered with. Sometimes scrutineers will react mid-season to a non-regulated tweak, banning for example the South African water-temperature sensor many folks ran in the Fiestas, because it allowed the coolant to circulate more effectively, having been designed for a hot climate. A better-cooled engine will generate slightly more power, leading to a speed advantage.

With the advent of electronic fuel injection and ignition, plug-in ECU checks have been implemented to make sure the engine map is to the regulated standard. This was a hot topic after the end of the 1999 Vectra Championship: one successful car was apparently sold to an unsuspecting racer after the last race who, on removing the carbon composite interior door panels, found a metal frame inside the door which was precisely the same dimensions as an ECU. What was it for? The whisper in the paddock was that it had enabled the driver to switch between the visible standard ECU and this alternative higher-performance unit once out on track, providing an advantage which may have explained his apparent straight-line speed.

Sometimes the enthusiasm of drivers to explain their lack of performance leads to such paddock rumours, which may or may not be substantiated and maybe are even intentionally encouraged. In the Autobytel Lotus Elise Championship, front-runner Adam Wilcox had his initials AW penned on several suspension components, easily visible to any casual observer. Were these components somehow different to ours, providing him with access to more advantageous set-ups? Or was this simply a stroke of psychological genius to destabilise his opposition? We will never know.

Things have moved on since then to a much higher level of sophistication. Scrutineers these days have to be highly knowledgeable and experienced detective engineers, able to identify for example the construction of an engine power restrictor plate which, when tightened into place, would deform to increase airflow to the engine, even if the plate itself appeared legal when removed. They have the authority to impound a car and strip it down directly from *parc fermé* after a race. This has driven engineers towards ever more creative solutions, including since-discovered flexible aerodynamic surfaces, on-track adjustable ride heights or cleverly hidden sources of nonstandard onboard fuel. Gone are the days of crudely replacing a fire extinguisher with a nitrous injection system, a trick I suspected one competitor of mine was using back in the Alfa Romeo days, after being passed up Clay Hill at Oulton Park as if I was standing still, only for that GTA to suddenly slow to my speed again, once ahead. Having said that, as racers, we'll always prefer a conspiracy theory if it can better explain why we were beaten!

PREPARE TO WIN

Assuming we have a car that has been prepared and set up as perfectly as possible, we also have to prepare ourselves as drivers. We are after all just another on-board system, albeit a fairly advanced one. If we are not operating optimally with the car, the result will be seen on the stop watch and on the faces of the team!

With my focus on endurance racing for the past 20 years or so, I have frequently driven different cars from season to season and the primary task is to get comfortable in the car. I don't even mean on the track; I mean in the workshop or pit garage. This human-machine interface underlines everything the driver will do in the car, so it all needs to become second-nature before blasting out of the pit lane. Of course, top-line modern race cars come with a driver manual and I will admit to poring over these ahead of time, but there is no substitute to actually sitting quietly in the car. As Steve McQueen's character Michael Delaney famously said in the 1971 film *Le Mans*, "When you're racing, it's life. Anything that happens before or after is just waiting." There is indeed a lot of waiting and we can make good use of that!

Initially, I'll familiarise myself with all the controls, starting with the indicators, wipers and headlight controls. It may sound mundane but these are the functions I'll need in a hurry and a selection error can be disastrous. A mis-signal at the Nürburgring 24 hours race for example, with around 150 cars on track, can result in a 'Nordschleife kiss', or even a full-blown relationship with the barrier!

Moving onto secondary controls, it's best to work with an engineer or team mate who is already experienced with the car. The goal is to run through a complete operating procedure, from start-up onwards, understanding the location and function of all switches and buttons on the steering wheel and dashboard. The level of complexity here is specific to each car, but endurance racers commonly offer multi-point adjusters for brake balance, ABS, traction control and stability control, along with other essentials including car-to-pit radio, pit lane speed limiter, fuel-reset button, headlight flash function and a very much appreciated drink button.

On top of this is the importance of becoming accustomed to the dash display and related controls which are an essential part of operating the vehicle and trouble-shooting problems on track. It's no use scrolling through unfamiliar pages mid-race, trying to find out where your fuel-used read out is located in response to a radio request from the pit wall. Getting to know these displays intimately allows rapid location or acknowledgment of a read-out without distraction. The 2023 Nürburgring 24 hours race provided a useful example: on the approach to Schwedenkreuz during my out lap, I radioed in with feedback that the Mathol Cayman had been uncharacteristically understeering through the Hatzenbach and Hocheichen corner sequence. Our engineer enquired what the front tyre pressures were. Thanks to our pit garage preparations, I could easily locate the correct data sub-screen on the run down through Fuchsröhre and report back at Adenauer-Forst where the radio signal improved again.

Lastly on the controls side are the emergency systems you hope never to need but if you do, it's vital to know where they are, even when you cannot see them. In the 2005 Silverstone 24 hours, I raced a Mazda RX-7 that abruptly lost all power during the night, leaving me stranded in pitch darkness between Club and Abbey corners. I needed to access ignition- and starter-switches by feel to try a re-boot procedure. I activated the hazard lights switch to avoid being hit on that very fast section (even though they didn't function) and ultimately could locate blind the door netting and release pull to allow me to exit to safety. A fire would have added an even further challenge, not only in terms of locating the extinguisher system button, but with smoke filling the cockpit, there would have been a lot less time available to get the hell out.

Now we are control-savvy, we can move onto the seat, the steering wheel and the pedals, the primary control touchpoints, all of which are of course permanently operated on track and need to be ergonomically ideal for the driver. Depending on the weight distribution of the car, it may first be helpful to consider where you want to position the seat, if this is not too limited by pedal travel and steering wheel reach. The seat itself, if shared with co-drivers, will simply be a shell, requiring inserts to be used to comfortably but firmly position the driver at the optimal height for confident visibility (even if it helps the centre of gravity to sit as low as possible), allowing easy operation of steering wheel lock-to-lock, gears and pedals, as well as clear sight of all displays. These seat inserts also help to keep the driver more securely positioned during a crash.

Rigid seat inserts moulded to the shape of the driver's body are a far better solution than cushions, very effectively transferring the various dynamic loads into the driver's sensitive posterior! Any movement between driver and seat delays this load transfer and consequently affects the reaction time and confidence of the driver. As Formula 1 driver Daniel Ricciardo commented, the driver and car need to act as a dance couple; I think that captures the required intimacy well. Back in 2019 at the Nürburgring, I shared the victorious #37 Aston Martin Vantage with Alex Brundle (then competing in LMP2) and Jamie Chadwick (of W-Series and subsequently Indy NXT fame). Aside from the age difference (their combined age was less than my own!), there was a huge driver height difference, for Jamie in particular. Her seat insert was about a foot thick underneath to raise her sight-line. To this day I don't know how she could be so competitive, balanced on top of such a massive insert!

The goal in any form of racing, whether sharing a car or not, is for drivers to be able to maximise their performance, not just over a single qualifying lap but more importantly over a full race distance where championship points are available. Exploring different driving styles to extract the most from the car is a further area of potential advantage, with benefits that are not always immediately obvious. Sticking with our 2019 Nürburgring 24 hours race Vantage example, Alex was our pace-setter, achieving super-quick lap times in the area of 8 minutes 57 seconds. However, to achieve this, he was using almost

13 litres of fuel per lap in contrast to a little more than 11 litres used on my laps that were only around two seconds slower. The telemetry revealed Alex's later, more aggressive braking (meaning he was on the throttle for longer), and lower gear selection through several corners (increasing revs and fuel usage). Maybe my older, more achy body prefers a smoother ride! In any case, these fuel-saving techniques opened up the possibility to extend race stints by an additional lap, before stopping for fuel. If every driver could have driven at that slightly more comfortable pace, maybe we could have eliminated one or even two three-minute pit stops over 24 hours, compensating for the two-second per lap advantage Alex was banging in! Different strategy, same outcome.

Fuel efficiency was not really a factor I considered seriously until a VLN race I was contesting in 2011. I was driving an Aston Martin V8 Vantage in the SP8 class. Nearing the end of the race, I was lapping as hard as ever, not realising I was staying ahead of the eventual top-class-winning car, and as a result I had to complete an unplanned additional lap after they finished. Subsequently, I ran out of fuel coming through Tiergarten, jumping out and pushing the car the last 200 metres (fortunately slightly downhill) to secure our podium finish. Hot slicks don't roll easily: fuelled by adrenaline, I practically collapsed behind the barrier after crossing the finish line. There is a video on You Tube entitled VLN1. Lauf 2011 "Wer seinen Wagen liebt, der schiebt," meaning "If you love your car, you push it." I did love that car but I resolved never to push it again!

By the way, I don't speak German particularly well, although it improves with a 'bier' or two, but learning the key words in the native language at the track is always helpful. There is a famous Nürburgring paddock story about a bus-load of guests calling their team to ask where the race track was. They had been driving around for hours, unable to locate the track. It turned out they were in Nürnberg, about 400km away from Nürburgring! A basic vocabulary of German racing terminologies also helps to make sure communications are clear between driver and team. In 2023, I caused quite some consternation on the pit wall when I let them know over the radio that there was no 'Wasser' in the car. Clearly, I meant 'Trinkwasser' in the drink system, not engine coolant water, but it took a few panicked exchanges to sort that one out. Mathol engineers and mechanics speak excellent English but I have raced for several other teams at the Nürburgring where it was German only.

Drinking during the race is actually something I thought of as a luxury for several years, and I initially forgot to make use of it when it was available. In fact, hydration has a major influence on concentration, as I have since learned, and I now make fluid intake a process triggered at least at one point every lap, not to mention part of my pre-stint routine. Racing by nature has some repetitive elements in the multiple laps we run around the circuit and this is a useful addition. Evidently, physical fitness and good nutrition also helps drivers to maintain energy levels which can mitigate concentration loss and fatigue. I've had the good fortune to get great guidance in this respect, not only from my daughter Beth, who has covered such topics within her Bath

University sports science degree, but also from other experts within the teams I've been fortunate to join. For example, John Camilleri of Boomerang Pro Fitness has supported Aston Martin Racing on many occasions, and during one race he was managing my nutrition and hydration, including a cocktail of specialist electrolytes. As I exited the car wild-eyed and still on fast-forward after a particularly crazy stint, he took one look at me and said, "Only water for you from now on!"

John's advice on caffeine intake was also useful: most of us enjoy a coffee or two but with all the interminable waiting around at race tracks, there is a temptation to over-indulge, with unhelpful caffeine crash consequences. The trick is to maintain the caffeine routine you are used to. The same applies to nutrition: stick with what works for you and don't suddenly start devouring specialist energy bars pre-race. There is nothing worse than suffering a bout of the gripes whilst out on track. For me, it's always a banana pre-stint. They contain natural sugars which are a good source of energy but their high-fibre content means they take a while to digest, delivering their energy over an extended period. And I can rely on the fact a banana is generally a banana, wherever I happen to be racing!

Of course, fatigue is also exacerbated by a lack of sleep. Night racing necessitates an interrupted sleep cycle and, like jet lag, it's something a driver has to get used to. I am fortunate in that I can fall asleep quite easily, at any time of night, even if I struggle to stay asleep for more than four or five hours. This is actually ideal for endurance racing, as the longest gaps between stints will never be lengthier than this. Nowadays, I make sure I have a hotel bed within reach of the track for the night breaks, a favourite example being the Dorint Am Nürburgring. The team has my mobile phone number and room number in case there is a change of stint time, so I can really relax. My first Nürburgring 24 hours race in 2003 was quite different: I was with an English team and we slept in our race suits in the back of the race truck behind the pit garage, so I used earplugs to minimise the noise. I remember being roughly shaken awake, some silhouette of a team member mouthing something at me. I pulled out an earplug and heard him yell, "He's comin' in!" Literally five minutes after being fast asleep, I was accelerating out of the pit lane to confront the Green Hell in the small hours of the morning!

I'll share an oddly similar sudden awakening a few years later, on a short French ski-break with a mate Charlie. He's a bigger drinker than I and he snores, so I would come back to our shared hotel room before him, stick the earplugs in and go to sleep. One night he came in very late, sozzled and needing a shower. He then came back out into the bedroom and leaned against the wall between our beds, accidentally hitting the main light switch. Shocked awake to the déjà vu of a male silhouette mouthing silently at me, this one was quite literally stark-bollock-naked! After an experience you can't unsee like that, a single hotel room seems a small price to pay.

Returning to endurance racing, maximising driver performance is then a key strategic component of success with many influencing factors. A further aspect is the desire of the drivers to be fastest within the team, a never-discussed but very real problem stemming from our sprint-racing backgrounds. There needs to be a very clear team management guideline regarding expected target lap times and the need to be 'in it to win it'. I tend to divide endurance events into three phases: Survive (until dawn), Consolidate (assuming survival!) and only then Attack (if it makes sense). Top-level multi-car endurance teams will advocate Attack, Attack, Attack with the expectation that they will lose cars along the way. Indeed, most of the major race-ending issues I've seen over the years have involved a departure from the Survive phase too early in the race. Contrary to the popular maxim, in endurance racing, it's the sunset that is full of promise and the sunrise that is full of knowledge.

The shorter the race, the shorter the Survival phase: in one-make sprints, only the first corner, maybe the first lap is about survival. Nevertheless, the secret to survival is similar in both sprint and endurance disciplines: it requires a significant observational talent to 'read' what the adjacent cars are about to do, positioning the car to avoid trajectories that will compromise progress or result in contact. This 'reading' is partly about understanding the laws of physics to the extent that it becomes clear where the car in front is headed by the attitude of the body, the angle of the wheels and line it has taken into the corner. As previously described, from a driver's perspective, race cars appear to move very slowly relative to each other, so there is time to take in a lot of information and anticipate their possible next moves. It's even possible to observe another driver's head position, to judge if your arrival has been noticed. Nevertheless, beware the unexpected: I raced a guy in Lotuses, and a few years later in British

GT, who confusingly insisted on deploying his indicators on the side he wanted us all to pass!

Raising the eyeline a little, there are other clues which can help to avoid disaster: for example, the speed or lines of the cars which are much further ahead, the crowd looking the other way down the track, are signals that should trigger a sixth sense, letting you know something it not as it should be. In 2014, at the wheel of the Aston Martin V12 Vantage for VLN #4, I was in a pack of Porsche GT3 Cup cars on lap one, thundering out of Hocheichen. Approaching the crest at Quiddelbacher Höhe, I saw a plume of dust against the trees above the blind Flugplatz corner. There was a spun Porsche on the exit and as the cars ahead braked heavily, I had to take to the grass, sliding unscathed through a Vantage-sized gap between the Porsche and the barrier. Let's face it, regardless of all driver anticipation skills, we all need a big slice of luck every now and again! As the Roman philosopher Seneca allegedly stated, "Luck is what happens when preparation meets opportunity." In some way, I was just about prepared enough to be lucky that day.

A further Survival phase tip is to be mechanically sympathetic to the car and to take only sufficient risk to remain in touch with any competitors ahead. Even if modern race cars are so much more robust, (especially when professional development drivers push them until they break), there are still risks, especially to the tyres and drivetrain, which can be mitigated by choices the driver makes. A pre-event track walk really helps here. At Spa, for example, understanding white lines and kerbs really helped lap times. When I first raced there in the Lotus,

I noticed when walking the circuit that parts of the track were denoted by the ultra-grippy Formula 1-specification white line, whilst other sections looked to have been painted back when the circuit was built in 1921! Knowing which could be utilised, especially in the wet, helped to reduce risk and was therefore a key competitive advantage.

Many more relevant fine details can be observed at walking pace, usually involving elements such as kerbs, painted white lines or concrete, astroturf, grass or gravel behind the kerbs which may cause a puncture or damage a drive shaft. There is so much invaluable knowledge to be gained and the process should be repeated every season because resurfacing and general track maintenance can alter kerb heights or remove other unhelpful features. I must admit, the evening before one Snetterton Fiesta race, my competitive nature got the better of me and I spent some time building up some of the larger gravel stones behind the sharp-edged chicane kerbs, allowing me to ride the apex with less risk of a puncture in qualifying the next day!

Even off the racing line, advantageous knowledge can be gained, including track surfaces and cambers, or temporary elements such as puddles or mud dragged onto the track, which would reduce grip when that section inevitably has to be used in the midst of traffic. In practice or qualifying, out laps or in laps are pressure-free opportunities to explore such extremes of track surface or kerbs.

Useful observations can also extend to macro-scale factors such as the prevailing wind direction which is much more obvious walking the track than peering at a weather map. At the Nürburgring, the almost 3km Döttinger Höhe flat-out section running all the way into

Tiergarten is a case in point. It runs more or less in a south-westerly direction but if for instance there is a prevailing headwind blowing slightly more from the south than the west, it is worth running in the lee of the left-hand barrier to gain some precious speed from the shelter it provides. Wind can affect corner speeds too: at Thruxton in the Fiesta, I could not understand why I seemed to have excessive understeer at Goodwood and Village corner in qualifying, despite trying various set-up changes to help me carry more speed. It was only in the evening when I walked the track, that I realised there was a fierce crosswind effectively blowing me off the track at the corner exit. The next day, the wind had changed, and magically in the race the Fiesta was glued to the track through there!

The same track later provided me with the opportunity to implement another great racing life-lesson from the legend Juan-Manuel Fangio who apparently said, "A lot of people would have beaten me if they had followed me." The first time I really benefited from this was by following Mark Cole at Thruxton. Mark was a seasoned instructor there and we were both racing in the Autobytel Lotus Sport Elise Championship, at least when the cars were reliable enough to allow it. In qualifying, Mark hung back in the collecting area and with all other cars on track, I pretended to have another issue with my car. Mark eventually departed and I followed. He couldn't hang back because the rest of the pack would have caught us and interfered with our laps. Running through the left-hand Noble into the right-hand Goodwood corner, I saw Mark's unique wide entry line and wow, how it changed the exit speed of Goodwood! In fact, when people say they don't brake for Church (the next very fast right-hander), I simply now respond, "Then you are screwing up Goodwood!" Those couple of laps behind Mark put me third fastest at that time.

I used the same 'follow and learn' tactic over 20 years later in the Köppen Motorsport Porsche Cayman at the Nürburgring. In this case, the track was not the issue. Rather, it was my lack of experience in that particular car other than a couple of qualifying laps. I was asked to take the start for our team and I decided to drop back to follow Christian Dannesberger, who had driven the team's sister car several times before. I saw his braking style, for example ABS flashing his rear lights, and understood the level of trail-braking he was using. A few laps in, I was able to pass him on the outside as he braked for the Kleine Karussell, to make sure I would get to the fuel stop first: if you come in for fuel right behind your sister car, you'll lose double the pit stop time!

Readying yourself to perform at your maximum as a race driver is then a complex business with many facets, both on and off the track. Each driver has unique strengths to be exploited and weaknesses to be overcome, and there is a wealth of experience available, particularly in endurance racing where there is a valuable culture of openness amongst co-drivers which is missing from most single-driver categories. Let me summarise it like this: prepare to learn, learn to prepare!

FIT TO RACE

Given the intense attention to detail associated with preparation of a winning race car, it's reasonable to expect that a serious racing driver would be at pains to be as physically and mentally fit as possible. There are many Sports Science experts who have researched and developed techniques for maximising physical and psychological human athletic performance. It's now quite common in professional motorsport to observe Performance Coaches working with drivers or other team members during or between race weekends. Back in 1989 however, it was quite an eye-opener for me to witness the limbering up routine of one of my most admired drivers, 'JJ Lehto', in the Oulton Park paddock before his Formula 3000 race.

My daughter Beth's pursuit of a career in this field of human performance in motorsport has taught me a lot that I wish I had known in my early racing years. It was a great help to work with her at the 2021 Nürburgring 24 hours race, to achieve and maintain an optimal level of 'aggression' for each of my race stints. Everyone has a different level of background 'arousal' which needs to be either enhanced or decreased, depending upon circumstance. For example, during the night besides a physical warm up routine, a carefully selected music playlist brought me from slumber to readiness, with a gradually increasing tempo to the point just before climbing into the cockpit. Once in that ideal zone, everything starts to 'flow', the car becoming the fabled extension of the body, doing everything I ask of it. I've experienced this euphoric state on more than a few occasions, driving with a rhythm where the car just seems to want to go quicker and quicker. It can make all the difference, even between team mates in the same car.

As with any one of us however, there are obstacles in the path towards this optimal mental 'flow' state. Most common for me have been sources of negative stress which handicap aggression with doubt. I have a life beyond racing. I have a wife and two daughters. Should I be doing this at all? Increasingly, I have to rationalise these thoughts and put them to one side every time I arrive at the track if I am to be competitive. This has nothing to do with my family's amazing support for my racing. It's the consideration that the risk may not be worth the reward, and consequently I have taken fewer risks in the latter part of my career than I did as a reckless 20-something-year-old with fewer responsibilities.

It is also a painful but accurate admission that I cannot be in the same physical shape as I was back then. My pre-race warm-up routine is more critical and I have to work harder to stay fit. You'll almost never see me in a gym though, unless I am travelling and unable to access the countryside. I'll even confess I get no kind of endorphin rush from lengthy physical exercise: it's all painful and I need rewards or distractions to maintain any kind of regular regime. When I was racing in the 1990s, I spent quite a bit of time on a mountain bike, sweating up the hills behind our house, my motivation being the fabulous twisting downhill return path through the woods, full of jumps and banked curves between the trees. God knows how I didn't injure myself...

I also used to cross-country run with an ex-Navy friend Lloyd who was maybe ten years younger than I. He was always keen to get out into the fresh air, maybe because he'd worked on nuclear subs under the Baltic ice for years. He'd literally run rings around me on the steeper hill sections, even if I took more risks on the descents to recover ground. I quickly worked out an effective strategy to slow him down: asking him simple questions that invited long answers to interrupt his breathing rhythm!

The most thrilling pre-season preparations I have enjoyed involved a very physical few days of snowmobiling in Michigan's Upper Peninsula with my Dow friends, Tom Shafer, John Lemanski and others. These machines were the start point for Gilles Villeneuve's racing career and they will do 100mph (160kmh) on the frozen lakes. I'm not sure what was more alarming, jumping over invisible ramps where the lake ice had cracked and thrust upwards, or skimming over sections that were definitely more water than ice! Steering the snowmobiles requires a good handful of throttle to slide the rear track and, on the narrow snowy trails, a big shift of body weight to keep the beast from rolling over. My sleds were borrowed or rented and in the latter case, the 'carbides' on the skis were usually worn out, meaning even more throttle to counter the extreme understeer.

On one particularly icy wooded S-bend, I overcooked it and, realising I was headed for the trees, I leapt off. Tom came around the corner to find a riderless sled vertical against a tree, a mark on the trunk about ten feet up (no metric in North America!) and no sign of me. I was buried deep in the snowy ditch! We managed to repair the sled (well to be honest, the tool we mainly used was a mallet) and thankfully the rental company folks were none the wiser.

A later escapade involved riding out to a beautiful log cabin restaurant and bar, where we enjoyed a classic steak and ale dinner. Tom had explained the trails would be prepared during the evening, so we'd have a wonderful smooth ride back. Around 10pm, I said to Tom that perhaps we should get going, as it was getting late. He looked quizzically at me and said, "Pete, don't you realise we are 150 miles away from home?!" We relished a stunning starlit ride back to his cabin, with all sorts of wildlife in our headlights. I've even seen wolves on the trails up there, but be warned if you try it: the temperatures can get so low, the mercury curls up into a little ball at the bottom of the thermometer. Thank heaven for heated handlebar mitts!

By far my best fitness investment though has been our vizsla Rocco. Tireless, always ready to go, he was a real lifeline through COVID-19 lockdowns. Since turning 45, every few years I've been obliged to perform a stress-ECG for my race licence and I can say on every occasion, with Rocco's help, I have consistently reduced my peak heart-rate on the treadmill. Have I maximised my fitness? Absolutely not. Is it enough to not be a source of negative stress at this stage of my career? Absolutely! Probably the greatest test of this was in 2011, when I had the privilege to race both of the only two Aston Martin V12 Zagato race cars in existence. Long before race car air conditioning was introduced, we had to endure cabin temperatures of 54°C! Despite exhibiting a face like a tomato, there was no physical impediment to my driving, at least as far as anyone could tell.

Physical injuries are also an increased hazard with age and I've suffered my fair share, but I'm fortunate never to have been seriously hurt in a road or racing car. Admittedly, I had a close call when asked to masquerade as the 'Stig' at the local village fete, a job that required opening proceedings with some stunts in a dune buggy. A week or so before, I went up to a farm field to practice some doughnuts and on that rutted surface, I managed to flip the buggy, trapping my leg underneath. Carrying a patched up bloody gash and severe bruising, I had to fly out to the States the next day. I met my boss in a Michigan hotel and as I limped towards him, I noticed he was limping too. For a second, I thought he was mocking my condition, but it turned out he had fallen off a pontoon boat about the same time I was rolling that buggy! The hardest aspect of this episode actually wasn't having to deal with my injury. It was having to play the 'Stig' all day, directly upon my return from the trip, whilst not being recognised by my two young daughters, as we had to keep my identity secret. The fact that the helmet of this 'Stig' was a size too small wasn't ideal either.

Going back to that Aston Martin Zagato, those with an automotive design interest would recognise its classically low roof line. What I recognised was the resulting intrusive roll-cage which meant I had to drive the race with my head tilted over to the right to avoid repeated whacks on the helmet over the bumps of the Nordschleife. Given a racing driver's essential use of balance to control the car, this was not an ideal driving position to achieve the desired 'flow' state! Worse still, my right shoulder seized up painfully as a result, making car control more difficult. Fortunately, John Camilleri was on hand again to help me bounce back with some expert physio attention between stints.

Thanks to a misunderstanding on my part at a very young age, this idea of balance was something I'd had in mind long before I ever started driving. I suppose I may have heard someone in motorsport talking about balance (of the car). Dreaming already of becoming a racer, I would literally balance on one leg on the edge of the bath tub for as long as possible, eyes shut for the most challenging test! In hindsight, I do believe these exercises, together with the mentioned foray into speed-skating, heightened my balance sensitivity and maybe even gave me some advantages in terms of feel in the car.

Ironically, years later in 2013, we were on a family holiday in the UK and after falling victim to a mystery affliction, I temporarily lost my balance altogether. It was the last day before we returned home and with the car packed, we went to bed, only for me to wake in the middle of the night, unable to control the position of my eyes or stand up. I literally crawled to the bathroom knowing I was about the throw up. I'll spare you the grisly details of the next very unpleasant few hours. Kim drove us home, my head over a crab-fishing bucket which distressingly smelled of rotting bacon! A head impulse test and suchlike with the GP was followed by several consultant appointments, a diagnosis of vestibular neuritis being the eventual outcome. I asked the specialist how I could have contracted this illness: he confided that although doctors typically describe it as a viral infection of the inner ear, no virus has ever been isolated. I can only say the enduring memory of that fateful evening packing the car was inhaling a strange-smelling scent from a plant growing next to our holiday cottage. Could that have been the cause?

In any case, I was in for many months of exercises to re-learn my balance before making a full recovery. Some of these had to be done in the hospital with the physio, with tests on specialist equipment which even a healthy person would struggle to master. Thankfully, other exercises were possible even whilst walking the dog. To illustrate just one of these, try walking rapidly along a straight line, shaking your head (as if saying no) with it tilted over towards one shoulder or the other at approximately 45 degrees. If your balance system is even slightly out of kilter, you'll fall off that line in a few steps. You may also appear somewhat alarming to passers-by! Even though I felt almost normal coming into the next race season, the first time back behind the wheel was certainly a nervous moment. Would approaching the limit expose persistent symptoms, limiting my capabilities on track? Thankfully not! I was able to set our qualifying time at VLN #4 and we took the same car to second place in the Nürburgring 24 hours race a month later.

Over the next few years, I was increasingly distracted by persistent lower back pain, a further source of negative stress which was relieved only by going out for a drive with the seat heater on full! I suspect it was the constant movement of the car that helped ease the pain but nevertheless I eventually had to have a scan to understand the problem. It turned out the discs between my lowest two vertebrae were almost completely collapsed. Fair enough, I've crashed a few cars in my time but nothing that should have led to this. The specialist gave me the jitters with his dire warnings of potential paralysis and this greatly played on my mind next time out as I braced myself over the bumps and jumps of the Nordschleife, really not the way to be at one with the car! I was therefore highly motivated to follow his recommended exercise routine (and have done ever since), to strengthen the muscles around the spine: three minutes of front-plank, followed by 90 seconds of side-plank (each side). I was pain-free within six months, I'm now comfortable in the race car and as a bonus, in a good light, I can even convince myself I've rediscovered my six-pack!

Neck-strengthening exercises also became a necessity over the years I drove with Aston Martin. Their cars were progressively quicker mid-corner, putting more g-forces on the driver's body. As we moved toward rigid moulded seat inserts mentioned in the 2am Prepare To Win chapter, I felt most of that lateral load on my neck. There were a few places that really exacerbated the problem, especially the very physical Turn 3 to Turn 6 sequence at COTA, or at the Nürburgring, the jarring bumps in the first kilometre through Hatzenbach and the bump at the left-right of the Spiegelkurve. Thankfully the 2019 resurfacing of the latter has eliminated the bump, making it a more rewarding and appreciably faster 'piff-paff' which also increases the entry challenge at the following 'Miss-Hit-Miss' multi-apex right!

For fellow-veteran racers with limited training time, I can recommend the 'Cato Combi-Workout' every morning! Balance in the side-plank position (both sides) and combine neck-strengthening lateral head raisers (with a neck harness if you wish) and leg raisers with mental agility tests (by reaching forwards to complete simultaneous hand-dexterity exercises of your choice).

The concept of combining mental exercise with physical training is very relevant to the role of a racing driver. Much of the physical activity of piloting the car is instinctive, but that does not mean it is subconscious. Every corner of every lap contains opportunities to further performance; if the process was subconscious, lapping would simply become a repetitive exercise with no gains made. Likely the driver would become complacent before being caught out by a change of track conditions. It's vital to be tuned into the huge range of visual, audial and physical inputs on track. The successful racer's brain processing rate is therefore very high, hence the illusory slow-motion effect described in 10pm It's About Time chapter. Like an old-fashioned slow-motion film playback, the film originally has to pass through the camera at high speed. It makes sense then to find ways to increase the brain's available processing capacity.

In recent years I have used mindfulness meditation for this reason. This practice focuses on the present moment, eliminating thoughts associated with potentially unhelpful past or future stresses. It's quite a commitment which initially requires sometimes painful confrontation and acceptance of anxieties and stresses, but the reward is the ability to better deal with them. With practice, it is possible to achieve a mindful state at will, once you have developed your own personal triggers. I find this particularly helps concentration and focus before I start the build-up towards the race start. Equally, with the need to get rest in between endurance race stints, I use the mindfulness 'body scan' and breathing techniques to calm my tensions without necessarily losing alertness, clearing the way to visualise the optimal outcome for the challenge ahead.

Like most training practices, it's up to the individual to discover what works for them. It's also true to say the routines need to change over time, depending on age and racing category of choice. If I was again at the start of my career, with the knowledge I have now, I would invest some time with a performance coach, establishing the appropriate mental and physical exercise protocols for my needs that season and beyond. I'd want to make sure I have a go-to expert, to ensure the inevitable times of crisis we all face at some point do not derail my championship campaign. At the very least, I'd want to be confident that I am maximising my capabilities in the car.

THE FEELING

Why is motor racing so addictive and thrilling, for drivers and fans alike? I believe the answer is rooted in the very ancient competitive nature of life itself, the compelling drive to survive which is present to varying degrees within us all. After all, every single one of us on this planet carries the genes of survivors.

In the civilised world, such base competitive instincts are often frowned upon, going against the equal opportunity policies of a caring society. Our competitive urges can then only be pursued in specific controlled environments, such as the sporting arena. This is nothing new: consider the huge popularity of the Roman gladiators, providing the civilian population with a taste of battle and reawakening their ancestral impulses. What I find interesting is the story of Flamma, a Syrian gladiator who won his freedom four times, but refused the *rudis*, the wooden sword that was the symbol of the gladiator's freedom. Perhaps he could not face returning to his destroyed motherland, ashamed of his defection to the Roman legions? In my view, it's more likely that he loved the thrill of combat, the feeling of victory and the recognition and status it provided him. I am sure giving it up was as unappealing as a driver giving up motorsport today.

The difference of course is that the race circuit is far more forgiving than the Colosseum would have been and so the thrill cannot be directly compared. Safety in professional racing has advanced enormously since the 1960s where grand prix fatalities were shockingly commonplace. Today, the danger appears remote, especially to the spectators with a shallow understanding of the sport, as evidenced by the distasteful jeers when a crowd-favourite's rival spins into the barrier. The expectation is that the driver will be just fine, but only a fool would assume so: any high-speed impact with an immobile object carries a high risk to the human on board. Racing on vast expanses of tarmac with no barriers would remove this hazard, but if all risk is eliminated, so to a large degree is the excitement and satisfaction for drivers and spectators. I suspect Flamma would not have been willing or able to entertain the crowds if he was armed with a harmless *gladius* made of foam. Of course, I am not endorsing added danger in motorsport, but there is a conundrum here that needs to be addressed, however uncomfortable.

Sports media rarely publicises that a key weapon in a driver's arsenal is the substantial fear of the consequences of a mistake, preferring instead to cultivate the stuff of legend. The movie Rush at least acknowledges James Hunt vomiting before his races, a nervous fear reflex which was very much at odds with his cool, playboy media image. That fear response he displayed is what allows every driver to operate at their optimum, perfectly balancing speed with the need to stay on track. This level of risk management is something largely missing in sim. racing, despite the impressive evolution of graphics and system dynamics. Real world crashes hurt both physically and financially. There is no reset button. Perhaps if sim. racers were knocked about a bit each time they crashed and their bank accounts were progressively relieved of all their cash, they might approach a sensation of fear closer to reality.

In reality, racing generates a stress response which many of us know as 'fight or flight'. If managed properly, this response brings a beneficial level of alertness and physical readiness to react. Too little stress and the driver may become complacent, the subsequent lack of concentration leading to under-performance or mistakes, like Ayrton Senna's famous 1988 Monaco Grand Prix crash whilst leading by a huge margin. Too much stress and the resulting panic-driven aggression will lead to a similar error-strewn outcome. I'd say this was perfectly exemplified in the first minutes of free practice at the 2023 Hungarian Grand Prix, when Sergio Perez, the subject of overwhelming media scrutiny that weekend, put a wheel on the grass approaching Turn 5 and crashed the car. Such a fundamental driving error would never have occurred under normal circumstances.

The 'fight or flight' response instantly releases adrenaline and endorphins, a relatively fleeting experience most of us recognise even from a young age when attempting a new and difficult accomplishment, leaving us afterwards with a euphoric feeling of survival success. I would hypothesise that motorsport extends this feeling far longer than nature intended, sometimes for hours in the case of endurance racing, the thrill being magnified as a result.

At a party some years ago, I spoke with a test pilot about precisely this notion. I was interested to know if the appeal of flying jet fighters at low altitude was down to a similar buzz and whether that stress response was an essential component for pilot survival. He agreed, but interestingly in a jet fighter, it's not about the enhancement of reaction times, but more about concentration and anticipation. In his world, as he unequivocally put it, "If you are reacting, you're dead!"

Anticipation is also a large part of driving a race car, providing vital confidence, even if the implications of failure are generally less severe than flying a jet. Lapping a circuit multiple times in a familiar car allows visualisation of any track section ahead of time, the anticipated forces on the car and body being the vital code for controlling the car before it gets out of shape. As discussed in the 12am The Limit chapter, an effective way to find the limit at a particular point is to exceed it, and then react quickly to bring the car back into line. However, with ingrained anticipation, this can be very difficult to put into practice, especially if the consequences are likely to include a trip into the barrier.

Bergwerk corner on the Nordschleife is for me a perfect example. This beast lies in wait under the trees just out of sight around the flat out 'Lauda Links' and is one of the most important corners on the track to get right, being followed by a 2.3km climb at full throttle up to the Mutkurve. The sequence approaching and beyond Bergwerk usually stays slippery even when the rest of the track is dry, due to the overhanging tree branches. The braking zone is very bumpy, slightly curved towards the turn in point and there is no run-off area in front of the barriers which extend around the corner and out of sight. The only helpful feature is the positive camber mid-corner, but even this can give a driver a false sense of security, as it quickly flattens on the corner exit, leading to a loss of lateral grip.

Despite the many hundreds of laps I have enjoyed at the 'Ring, Bergwerk certainly peaks my fear levels every time. I cannot find the limit by exceeding it, so I need to creep up on it, every lap pushing a few centimetres further into the invisible psychological wall that represents the braking point, but all the while very aware that conditions could have changed since I was last there, eight to nine minutes previously.

In some cases, this mental barrier is not only a fleeting phenomenon on approaching such 'monster' corners. It can also pervade a driver's psyche in the pit garage. In 2021, with Köppen Motorsport in the Porsche Cayman, our sister car driven by Stefan Branner went off in tricky conditions at Tiergarten, another of the Nordschleife's most ruthless sections, approached at over 170mph (275kmh). His car mysteriously speared left into the barrier before bouncing and flipping across to the right-hand side of the track. Thanks to the structural strength of the Porsche, the immediate attention of the track safety crews and the doctors in the local hospital, Stefan made a full recovery. Nevertheless, seeing the team's other car, previously identical to the one we were driving, but now almost unrecognisable with every panel smashed, certainly caught my attention. Those tiny doubts creep in and have to be quashed with clear rationale before getting back behind the wheel.

Quite a few drivers won't race on the 'Ring as they perceive it to be too fearsome and dangerous. Without wishing to sound foolhardy, that's a part of why it has so much appeal over almost all other race tracks around the world and why I am addicted to driving there! There are no posers at the 'Ring: every driver who continues to compete there is doing it for the enormous gratification it provides, being well aware of the risks involved to trigger that response. It requires many years of practice, patience and a fair share of accidents, to really begin to build up sufficient confidence and to appreciate the wizardry of the Gustav Eichler-designed Nordschleife (not forgetting the since abandoned Südschleife). It is fortunate indeed that the track was built back in 1927; I am quite sure a modern-day planning application for such a track would be turned down.

Fear and confidence are then two key components controlling and optimising speed; they work against each other to achieve a kind of equilibrium which could be defined as a comfort zone. This can be enlarged for example by driver experience, by the support of the team or fans of the team, by the presence of other competitors on track and even by the expectation of a rewarding dopamine release! There have been some situations where I have had to go well beyond my comfort zone. One that is still alarming to recall was the Lotus Sport Elise Championship event in the torrential rain at Spa, where we were driving flat out on the Kemmel straight with no forward visibility other than the windscreen wiper against a grey opaque background. I was literally watching the side of the track, looking for the Les Combes corner markers: 300, 200, 100, brake! With vision deprived, other senses even came into play, for example listening for the car ahead to back off for the approaching corner. Why would we put ourselves through that experience? To win of course and to survive a great challenge! Practically, there was also the concern that running at slower speeds could lead to someone running into the back of the car, but I suspect that was more an excuse than a justification!

In theory, age should eliminate the ignorant recklessness of youth. A fast older driver could perhaps be described as more courageous, as they better understand the consequences of their actions but still elect to continue with the pedal hard down. Experience has a lot to do with this: "It worked out before so it'll work out again." I can confirm more than 20 years after that Lotus race, in the fog and darkness of the 2021 Nürburgring 24 hours, I applied exactly that same Spa method of watching the trackside and listening for other cars, the Cayman's usual speed hardly altered up to an invisible Schwedenkreuz. I will admit though, I was relieved a few minutes later to get the radio call that the race had been red-flagged due to poor visibility; perhaps after so many years of racing, my self-preservation instincts need to be reset!

Everything is relative, of course. My exploits at the 'Ring may seem excessively dangerous to some, but to me it is a safer proposition than driving on public highways where traffic approaches from all directions, often driven with questionable skills or attention, in cars with no roll cages, no six-point harnesses or on-board fire systems, on roads with few barriers, no gravel traps, no flag marshals or immediate rescue services. Yet the risks of public roads are an acceptable part of everyday life for many people.

What appears to be an insane level of danger in my eyes is the Isle of Man TT. I'm simply not equipped to understand the confidence those riders can feel on their bikes in that environment. Kudos to them! Fear would dominate that experience for me and prevent any hope of a competitive showing. Nevertheless, just like an excess of fear, too much confidence is not helpful. Clearly driving with caution won't win any championships, but an over-confident driver soon ends up in the wall.

It's important then for drivers to surround themselves with realists, either team members or other close friends, who can help keep the fear and the confidence in balance, especially over a long season of ups and downs. A motor race produces one winner and a whole bunch of losers and it's difficult to maintain confidence when things aren't going your way. The long gaps between races can be absolute torture, especially if the driver feels the team is not sufficiently supportive. The after-effects of a poor race performance may not only be seen in the loss of championship points, but also loss of reputation, perhaps loss of sponsorship backing and ultimately even loss of the race seat. Even top-level Formula 1 driver careers have suffered these consequences, their confidence destroyed by shocking treatment from teams who should know better.

Counter-intuitively, confidence can also come from having a quick team mate. Bear with me on the logic here. It may be tempting to join a mid-field team where you can be quick in comparison to your team mate, but in reality, you'll then be fighting everyone else in the field with no clarity on how they are achieving their success. If your team mate is the quickest driver in that field, in theory they are the only one you'll need to beat, you'll be in the same well-prepared and competitive car (at least you should be) and incredibly, you'll likely have access to their telemetry and set-up! A bad weekend would be finishing second!

Through endurance racing, I've had the privilege to drive cars with some absolutely world-class team mates, including Nicki Thiim, Darren Turner, Jonny Adam, Alex Lynn, Vincenzo Sospiri and others already mentioned. I've seen how they operate, how they interact with the team, how they drive the car, where the differences are between us, and I have been able to up my game as a result. Even in my 'veteran' years, their help has meant I can still lap very close to their times. It's a case of 'mind over motor' to some extent: when you see their telemetry data with a later braking point or higher mid-corner speed for example, it allows a recalibration of your own fear-confidence balance, with satisfying results. I still recall Nicki's excitement in 2017, when he congratulated me after I emerged from my initial Nürburgring stint in the Vantage GT8 we were sharing for the first time: he had just realised we had a real opportunity of victory together!

The feeling of driving a properly set-up race car close to its limit has not really changed over the decades I've been competing. Electronic driver assistance systems can get in the way somewhat, but if you are quick, all the same sensations are still there. Skilful use of throttle, brake and steering to distribute longitudinal or lateral load between the tyres whilst anticipating the point of declining grip is still intrinsic to racing success in any category. When we superimpose the more instinctive, primeval responses mentioned in this chapter, we can unlock all our capabilities to become a more complete racing driver.

SUPERSTITIONS & PREMONITIONS

As the 4am The Feeling chapter reveals, confidence is a key ingredient for racing success, with many rational foundations for the driver's belief in the car, in the team and in their own abilities. There are also many irrational beliefs, habits and practices which are very personal and not usually discussed publicly or amongst drivers, either because it may be perceived as a weakness to be exploited, or may simply be embarrassing to admit! On the face of it, such things can appear quite amusing to onlookers, but if interfered with, can significantly destabilise the driver's performance.

Even pre-season, there is the choice of car number for example. In my case, it was important to secure #7 for my Fiesta and Vectra years. Why? It just felt right! It was only years later I found out about Stirling Moss's superstitious belief in this number and how he won around half of all the races he contested with it. In 2000, as #7 was already taken, I added a 1 in front of the 7 for my disastrous #17 Lotus Sport Elise campaign: maybe there was something in lucky #7 after all!

Apart from that Lotus, I've almost always competed in cars with the driving position on one side or the other, so I've never had to contend with the superstition that stepping into the car should always be done from the same side. The engineers and mechanics would have found it perplexing indeed if I had tried to wriggle across to the driver's seat from the passenger door!

It's entirely reasonable that a driver develops a close relationship with a specific car, given the intimacy and feeling involved in successfully piloting the machine to victory, not to forget the narrow escapes shared along the way. Some drivers or engineers have been known to talk to their race cars, bringing them to life at least in their own minds. I can't say I've ever had a meaningful dialogue with a car, but I will admit to the odd yell of encouragement when trying to slipstream past another competitor, or a congratulatory pat on the dashboard of our road car after completing a long and arduous journey!

Some drivers have historically considered a green car to be unlucky. Perhaps this sentiment was rooted in early historical references to green clothing being ill-fated in a variety of cultures. I think it's far more plausible that this myth was borne out of some early high-profile auto-racing accidents involving green-painted cars. For me those cars could equally well have been red or blue! The location of the accident is far more meaningful than the car colour. For example, several bad races at Brands Hatch meant it became a bit of a bogey circuit for me. In any case, no colour choice concerns stood in the way of British Racing Green or other similar shades widely-used for over a century by famous marques including Aston Martin, Bentley, Jaguar, Lister, Lotus and others.

Continuing along the green theme, the Green Hell has its own odd superstition, one that I find little trace of outside the Nürburgring paddock. During one of the many 'steak-on-a-stone' meals I have enjoyed in the local Pistenklause restaurant, I was told, as a driver, you should never visit Nürburg castle, the brooding 12th century ruin that overlooks the Nordschleife, or bad luck with befall you! I've enjoyed exploring many ancient castles in my time and the view from the one at Nürburg must be stunning. I may be relatively old amongst racing drivers, but I still have a few races within me, so I'll save that particular expedition for after I've retired from racing!

Amusingly, my family refer to my 'OMP' fireproof underwear as 'Old Man's Pants'. I've never been a part of the 'lucky underpants' club though. Apologies for the mental image but you shouldn't wear underpants at all beneath your fire-proofs: they just make you hotter and if made from nylon or polyester, would probably melt in a fire. I did use to be somewhat fussy about my Nomex socks. They had a label on one side or the other, and I preferred to have a 'balanced' pair! Did anything bad happen when the labels were both on the same side? Of course not! It's just didn't feel right. These days, I intentionally pick out my socks randomly, out of defiance to superstition! Unlike Alex Wurz, I'm not obliged to wear odd-coloured race boots either, but I do feel unprepared if I don't tuck the laces inside my bootstraps.

My main priority is comfort. Any wrinkle or seam in race underwear can be a distraction in a hot, sweaty driver's seat, especially with the multiple-belts and HANS devices all pressed tight against the body. I've heard that some driver superstitions won't allow them to shave on the morning of a race: personally, I really dislike how a Nomex balaclava snags on an unshaved chin, so shaving is part of my routine, sometimes even between stints in a 24 hour race!

On an even more personal note, for most of my racing life, I have worn a small silver Celtic cross my mum gave to me. In fact, I was surprised at how gutted I was when I lost the original somewhere in the Thruxton mud. I think my reaction was rooted in my early days when Dad would fix to the dashboard a small Saint Christopher, the patron saint of travellers and motorists. That small badge and my Celtic cross both felt like a psychological safety net, a protective device which in part provided a basis for my racing confidence. It was really important to find the replacement that I've worn ever since. I can sympathise with any driver who carries or wears such a talisman, even if the FIA International Sporting Code looks to ban the wearing of metal jewellery.

I recognise here that religion has long been a powerful force for racing drivers. Like the warriors of history, they charge into battle to win trophies and their religious convictions can be just as important. It's quite common to see a finger pointing heavenwards on any podium in acknowledgement of a higher power's guidance or protection. Honestly, that's not how I see it, even if I have had personal experiences of what could be higher power interference. When I was a young schoolboy for example, my prized possession was a model yacht, that one windy day became stuck deep in a reed bed, far out in the middle of the mystical Llyn Dhu ('Black Lake') at Lindow Common in Cheshire. It was too far and too dangerous to swim out to recover it, so as nobody was around, I did what years of Christian school education prompted in times of need: I said a prayer. When I opened my eyes, my boat was sailing directly towards me having apparently extracted itself from the reeds, the wind miraculously changed.

I was quite willing to believe God intervened that day, but when it comes to motorsport, I find it unlikely that such a fair-minded power would provide a competitive advantage to certain drivers. Let's not even discuss whether a driver of one religion would have a greater advantage than an equally devout proponent of another! I wear the Celtic-cross partly because Mum has Welsh blood and gave it to me, but also because I see it as a symbol of tolerance between belief systems. It's preposterous that humans fight over religions which were originally devised to prevent anarchy and violence within our societies and cultures. I believe there is, after all, only one human race, simply divided by location.

What I also struggle to explain are what might be called paranormal occurrences, premonitions that have had a direct impact on my actions, both in the car and elsewhere. Clearly embracing a topic such as this risks plausibility! However, I have realised from various discussions over the years that I am not alone in these experiences. As with most areas that are little understood, dialogue brings enlightenment, so I'll start here!

The date was Wednesday 6th March 1991. Dad and I were testing the red Class C Alfasud at Mallory Park, and I had driven up from my student house in Coventry that morning to meet him there. We had decided to uprate the front brakes and the test was mainly for me to get used to them. Mallory Park in those days was fast track with no Charlies or Stapletons bends. We'd carry a lot of speed out of Gerards and there was also no Edwina's chicane at the end of the Stebbe Straight: the little 'Sud would exit the John Cooper Esses a little over 80mph (130kmh). A slight curve left over the brow and the driver was confronted with the tight right-hand Shaw's Hairpin, a great location to try out our new brakes, if somewhat daunting with its steep grass bank and barrier directly ahead of the braking zone.

That day was sunny and dry. I had been confidently building up speed without any problem, but as I hit the brakes for Shaw's the pedal went to the floor. I pumped at it, but the car was not decelerating and the fearsome barrier was fast approaching. Almost on autopilot, I glanced down to the floor of the car and yanked the handbrake so hard, I broke the cable in an attempt to rotate the car. Just before the impact, having never experienced a major crash before, I remember thinking, 'This is it!'. Of course, it wasn't. Given the high speed of the crash, the car was pretty badly stoved-in on the front left corner, but I was fine thanks to the safety equipment doing its job. It later turned out a front brake pad had jumped out of the calliper, having not been securely fitted.

A brake failure such as this is every driver's nightmare. The curious fact is, it *was* precisely my nightmare five days previously! In the early hours of Friday 1st March in Coventry, I dreamt the whole sequence with Mallory Park in every detail, from the moment the brake pedal went to the floor. I even saw the sunlight on the red floor of the 'Sud and I am quite sure I would not have had the presence of mind to pull the handbrake, had I not somehow already done so previously. Back in the pit lane, Dad simply said, "Make sure you tell me next time you have a dream like that!"

I drove back to Coventry questioning the whole episode and my sanity. Along the way, I realised there was a foolproof method to determine the truth of the matter. As soon as I arrived, I said to Nick, my housemate, "Do you remember the dream I told you about last Friday at breakfast?"

He replied, "You mean the one where you crashed the Alfasud?" That was all I needed to hear, to confirm I wasn't going crazy!

On occasion, over a pint or two with friends, I've tried to understand this phenomenon. The discussion usually leads down the path where time is maybe not the linear construct we know, stitched together with one second following another on the clock, to allow us to make sense of what we call reality. Maybe instead, everything is interacting all at once in parallel planes, and perhaps if our brains are receptive, we can pick up major event disturbances across those planes. I'm painfully aware at this point that my credibility is fragile! I can only point to history, where any given society has only been able to judge their experiences through their own frame of reference; later generations, with the benefit of new learning, can easily see past those constraints. Perhaps the same will one day be true of my inauspicious Mallory Park dream.

Years later, travelling from Stansted Airport on business, I encountered a different type of premonition. Despite travelling more than a hundred thousand business air miles, I have in recent years developed a minor fear of flying. Like most drivers, I am of course a bad passenger in any case, but in the early days I was relatively unconcerned about taking to the skies. That is until I arrived at the gate in Stansted in the mid-1990s. Anyone who has used that airport will know the gates are reached by an underground train: all was smooth to that point, but as soon as the train doors slid open, I felt something was wrong. It wasn't much at first, but as I climbed the escalator and approached the gate, there was a physical reaction, cold sweats and an overwhelming sense of foreboding. I actually didn't know what to do. Should I try to convince the gate staff that something may be wrong with the plane, potentially averting disaster for the hundreds of passengers? Or should I take the coward's option of fabricating a reason to abandon the flight, leaving everyone else to their fate? Before I had to make that appalling decision, the airport tannoy announced there was a technical issue with the plane and we would all be bussed to Gatwick for a replacement flight! Needless to say, I drove straight home.

Even if these experiences provided some illusion of clairvoyant capability, I don't have a radar for the future. There have been many more instances where I wish I had been able to predict a critical outcome, but clearly did not, otherwise I'd be a lottery winner! Notwithstanding my Stansted reaction, I don't even have certainty that anything untoward would have happened that day, even if it may have in some parallel dimension. I simply find it fascinating that these phenomena cannot be properly explained, especially given my long participation in a sport where risks are ever present, where self-belief is a fundamental component of success and where time is certainly defined by one second following the other!

THE QUICK & THE DEAD

This chapter is dedicated to the drivers I have known personally, who sadly lost their lives on the track. I have carefully considered the content here because my primary concern is to show the greatest respect for these people, their families and their accomplishments. At the same time, the authenticity of this book can only be preserved if we do not ignore this controversial topic.

There are some extreme sports competitors who believe the risk of dying gives more meaning to life. They seem need that level of danger to achieve their 'buzz'. In all my racing years in the modern era, I have never encountered a driver who was motivated by exposure to the risk of injury or death. Even including the much more perilous former years of motorsport, part of the driver psyche has always been to suppress such thoughts, operating under the illusion that 'it won't happen to me'.

Nevertheless, as the entry ticket states, 'Motorsport Can Be Dangerous' and not a race season goes by without a reminder of this fact somewhere around the world. Even those who were not dedicated fans of the sport were deeply touched by the shocking loss of Williams' Ayrton Senna on that fateful 1994 weekend at Imola. Ayrton, for me as for many others, was a hero and was also the reason that yellow featured prominently in my early helmet colour schemes. His apparent combination of talent and humanity transcended the sport, touching many around the world. It was equally appalling that Roland Ratzenberger should lose his life in qualifying the previous day. I never actually met Roland, but I had watched his early career racing Formula Ford and British F3, as well as BTCC in a BMW M3. It was this familiarity with him and the tracks he'd raced upon that struck hard.

Nevertheless, difficult as it may be to accept in the modern world, the risks involved in motor racing elevate the feats of the participants, just as a circus high-wire performance is elevated by the absence of a safety net. The willingness of the performers to literally put their lives on the line, relying purely upon their skills time after time, may be incomprehensible to normal society, yet it always draws a crowd.

For the keen competitor, there is certainly a direct correlation between risk and reward. Take for example an experienced poker player going all in: they've judged the odds to be worth it, but regardless of whether they actually win, there is a tremendous thrill associated with that moment of risking it all. If that same poker player was restricted by a house rule to small bets, they would probably choose to play somewhere else. In a nutshell, that's a good analogy to explain my two decades and more racing at the Nürburgring Nordschleife. It's a high-stakes poker table and whether we win or not, we come away with a tremendous sense of achievement.

In motorsport generally, the odds have moved in our favour when it comes to safety, thanks to the amazing work by the various organising bodies, originally in response to pressure from the Grand

Prix Drivers Association. I had been racing for almost ten years in the UK before I was present when a fatality occurred. I was racing the Vectra at Oulton Park and remember standing at the fence of the collecting area watching a very promising Irish driver named Neil Shanahan in the works Van Diemen prepare for the fifth round of the 1999 British Formula Ford Championship. Three cars tangled at Clay Hill a few minutes later and he was gone. He was 19 years old.

Drivers each process such an accident in their own way and inexplicably for some, they take to the track nonetheless. I can only speak for myself in this regard. I frequently thought about Neil every lap I drove up Clay Hill, much as I think about Niki Lauda every time I negotiate the left-hander where he endured his fiery Nürburgring crash. It's a stark reminder that what we do is not to be taken lightly, and that respect between competitors on track is paramount if we are all to come through unscathed.

The problem however with increasing safety is that drivers simply take more risks. Just a few weeks before Oulton Park, we had been racing the Vectras at Thruxton, where Rob Collard had a monster high-speed shunt into the tyre wall before the chicane. The car was destroyed but thanks to the roll cage and other safety equipment, Rob emerged unhurt and was racing a new car at the next event. Witnessing such accidents lead other drivers to believe they are indestructible and the quality of driving inevitably declines. The same outcome is evident with the removal of track features which are considered to be dangerous. Take for example Eau Rouge-Raidillon or Pouhon corners at Spa, the old trackside gravel being replaced by immense tarmac run-off areas. Drivers could attack these corners far more aggressively than previously, expecting only a track limits penalty if they got it wrong. In my opinion, this simply replaced one safety issue with another.

To make progress, it's important to understand why accidents happen. The reasons can essentially be covered by four categories: car failure, driver error, grip loss (that is not caused by driver error) and miscommunication between drivers.

Car failure is essentially an engineering and preparation matter but as we've seen, mechanical sympathy on the part of the driver can also play a major role in avoiding such an accident. My budget-conscious club racing background taught me especially to look after the engine and gearbox, a failure of either potentially spinning the car into the barrier on its own oil. Having disassembled my Vectra gearbox mid-season, I recall Barwell commented the internals looked like new, thanks to careful heel-and-toe and clutch application. Mechanical sympathy can also be as simple as tyre preservation on an abrasive track such as Thruxton, where drivers must restrain themselves in the early laps if a later tyre blow out is to be avoided. Punctures are never pleasant, generally cost a lot of time and can damage the car on the way back to the pits even if the driver has avoided an accident by quickly reacting to the deflating tyre.

More serious are suspension or brake failures which are generally instantaneous, causing for example the famous loss of both front wheels on Sebastien Buemi's Torro Rosso in practice for the 2019 Chinese Grand Prix. In 2015, I was reunited with Chris Harris and

Oliver Mathai as team mates in the Aston Martin GT12, together with very quick Nürburgring local legend Andy Gülden. Andy was pushing hard in the dawn stint of the 24 hours when one of the brake ducts became blocked with debris. The brake disc overheated and abruptly failed, pitching Andy into a massive shunt at Bergwerk and ultimately into hospital, fortunately with no lasting injuries.

At the same track in 2009, I raced a CK35 RS Mercedes, run by Brückner Motorsport. One of my team mates was experienced Japanese driver Yasushi Kikuchi, who drove a race stint ahead of me. Yasushi radioed in with an understeer issue on right-hand corners but when I climbed in, I immediately found the handling problem to be severe. It later turned out the car had taken quite a knock, but this was not communicated to me. Up through Klostertal on my first lap out, I turned in to the long right-hander and the steering just broke, sending me straight into the barrier. Fortunately, I could rotate the car a little on the brakes and the impact was more-or-less broadside. Had the failure occurred at another location, the outcome could have been a lot more serious.

You might say this accident should be attributed more to driver error than car failure, after Yasushi's earlier impact and with me pushing what in hindsight was a damaged car. In fact, driver error usually plays at least some part in the majority of accidents. Even though my high-speed accident at Kesselchen in the Aston Martin GT8 could be categorised as grip loss, it was the result of fitting slicks whilst the track was wet (see the 11pm Tell It Like It Is chapter) and also my driving error by improperly compensating my speed for the slippery track conditions. Pure grip loss accidents are thankfully rare and can only be attributed to a sudden decrease of surface grip with no warning to the driver, such as a fluid leak on the track for example which is not visible and not (yet) signalled by the trackside marshals.

The last accident category is miscommunication between drivers that can result in an accident even for the innocent party. It's a subject frequently discussed in driver briefings and yet it happens all too often, especially in events where there are multiple classes with different speeds and cornering abilities all running together. In that environment, a driver needs to be able to differentiate between those in the same class and those in a faster class. It's another level of detail compared to one-make racing, where the mirrors are essentially a part of a driver's peripheral vision, to be aware of any threat from other competitors. Beyond traditional mirrors and blue flag signals, there are various other systems available to help. One of the most effective was fitted to our 2019 Vantage, comprising a rear-view camera and dash-mounted screen which gave a live indication via red or green highlighting whether the car behind was closing in or not. It was a fantastic tool which in my opinion should be mandatory for multi-class racing.

At the Nürburgring, the SP9 GT3s and other front-running cars also carry a flashing blue light in the windscreen which, like the *polizei*, encourages the cars ahead to pull over. In fact, that is one of the worst things to do: a car being lapped should stay on the racing line, avoiding any unpredictable behaviour. It's up to the approaching car to find the safest way past; after all they have the better view. One more tip:

those GT3s often circulate in groups of two or three, so if you are letting one through into the braking zone, always check for others before you turn in!

Sometimes accidents between cars are just inexplicable. In 2023, I came up behind a BMW 328i approaching Hohe Acht. Rather than dive through on the brakes, I waited for the short straight before Wipperman to pass him safely on the right-hand side. As the trackside footage shows, our Porsche was at least half a car ahead, but the BMW driver still turned in, bouncing off my rear quarter panel. I'd left lots of space, felt the contact, then saw him in my mirror crashing heavily into the barrier, luckily with no serious consequences to the driver. He knew I was there but had followed his normal line as if sleepwalking.

It is this kind of unpredictable behaviour that causes the most serious accidents. In 2010, I was in my first year with Aston Martin, driving the V12 Vantage. Also in the team, driving a GT4 Vantage, was Prince Carl-Friedrich of Löwenstein-Wertheim-Rosenberg, or Leo as he liked to be called. At the infamous Bergwerk corner, Leo was in a collision with two other cars. His car hit the guardrail and overturned, sustaining massive damage at the rear and bursting into flame. Although medics and marshals were able to get to the car immediately, Leo was trapped and he died of smoke inhalation there by the track as the race was red-flagged. Despite my earlier comments about this being a high-stakes game, it was of course deeply saddening that this could happen to such a straightforward, friendly and popular man. I'll never forget how moving I found team mate Richard 'Dickie'

Meaden's later words, describing Leo's neatly folded clothes waiting in the driver changing room we all shared.

We can take some comfort from the fact that Leo was doing the sport he loved when he died, but the reality it brings home is that it can happen to anyone, even if drivers wilfully convince themselves otherwise. At Tertre Rouge during the early stages of the 2013 Le Mans 24 hours, the freak impact of Allan Simonsen, one of the best, was another close-to-home example. Just a few weeks before, we'd been chatting in the pit garage and, like Leo's accident, I felt somehow guilty that my desire to continue racing was not weakened by these catastrophes befalling our team mates.

I've since understood that we continue race in their honour: to stop would be in some way to diminish the worth of their achievements. It is no accident that the media often report a 'duel' or a 'battle' between motor racing protagonists. The analogy is clear, the implication being that the consequences of engagement can be extremely serious, sometimes even fatal. In this context, I remember those drivers in these pages, their fellowship, their exploits and their courage.

RACE-CRAFT

With 20, 30 or even 150 cars all vying for the same racing line, there are always going to be incidents between drivers on track which are questionable. Stewards judging such incidents follow the FIA International Sporting Code (or equivalent), a set of sporting and technical regulations which are carefully written and updated to try to make sure racing is fairer and less dangerous. However, there is a significant amount of discretion placed in the hands of the stewards. As the FIA stated when publishing their Driving Standards Guidelines, these are 'merely guidelines to assist the stewards in their decision making and are non-binding'.

In the early 1990s, it was rare for our racing to be televised, and as such, judgments regarding the on-track action depended upon observers (usually marshals) at each corner, who would submit a report when there was an accident or an altercation between cars. These reports were collected and used in evidence by the Clerk of the Course after the race, but they could be wildly inaccurate. I know on at least one occasion an observer's report referenced a car number which was not even in the race! Consequently, drivers then could get away with a lot which today would be picked up by trackside and on-board television, as well as telemetry data showing steering, brake and throttle positions.

Take for example those front-wheel-drive one-make categories I raced in the first decade of my career. In order to help their 'turn in' into corners, just like the equivalent BTCC cars today, the rear of the car was set up to be very 'light'. On a clear track, the driver could intentionally destabilise the rear with the steering, especially under heavy braking, to help rotate the car towards the corner apex. Now bring into the picture a car behind, that second driver allowing a light contact with the braking car ahead. It's not difficult to achieve: as both cars brake, the following car slightly eases the brake pressure as they approach the turning-in point. It looks like nothing from the trackside, but if the tyres are already on the limit of adhesion, the car ahead is easily tapped into a spin or slide, or at the very least the required opposite steering lock runs the car wide through the corner on a non-ideal line, sapping speed and allowing the following driver to simply drive by at the corner exit. Such 'hits' still frequently occur under the mantra 'rubbing is racing', especially in the melee of the first lap where observers' vision is often obscured by the traffic.

A more malicious version of this move targets disabling of the car in front, either by damaging the exhaust, rear suspension or diffuser, or by pushing the rear bumper or bodywork onto the tyres. As you've read, this happened to me on my BTCC debut at Brands Hatch in the Barwell Honda at Graham Hill bend, forcing a costly pit stop for rear bumper repairs.

Progressing further into the corner, we need to consider the ideal lines which allow the car to maximise speed in each section. Let's take the first half of the corner up to the apex and imagine those same two cars following each other. Normally both cars would take a wide line on approach to open up the corner (increase its radius) and carry more speed through as a result. On this occasion the car behind has not nerfed the rear of the car in front, but instead decided to take a dive down the inside in the braking zone, on a tighter than normal line. This is a classic out-braking manoeuvre which, even if the tighter line makes things more challenging, should be executed without contact. On this occasion, the overtaking car impacts the side of the other competitor's car. The rules of conduct here generally state that if the overtaking driver has a significant portion of their car alongside, then the other car should expect to surrender the corner. The inside car's priority then becomes to get alongside by the apex, rather than to avoid contact, even using the car ahead as a bit of a brake should they continue to turn in towards the apex.

This type of incident happens at all levels, and especially in the case of open-wheel categories, it can result in dangerous tyre-to-tyre contact. There is clear guidance in drivers' briefings about leaving a car's width for other competitors, both in the braking zone on either side if you have moved across to defend a corner and also if you are rejoining the racing line. This is of course to avoid crashes caused by contact where there is an overlap between the rear of the leading car and the front of the overtaking car. A famous example was the altercation that blew up social media, between Max Verstappen and

Lewis Hamilton at Silverstone's Copse corner, in the 2021 edition of the British Grand Prix. Lewis got up alongside but there was no way he could make the corner on that line with Max taking up track space and so, too late, he lifted out of it. The cars made contact and Max was spun into the wall.

Leaving a car's width is a rule that can be exploited, primarily by forcing the overtaking car onto the less grippy parts of the track. This can be risky if they are attempting to pass on the inside as we may inadvertently end up with their front bumper in our door (or nose in our side-pod if you prefer): we have to watch our mirror and be ready to take avoiding action. It's a fine balance: we need to ensure any modification to our line will not cost us more speed compared to our adversary.

A more effective defence method is to force the other to pass on the outside and if necessary, run slightly deeper into the corner towards the apex. This prevents the car behind from driving around the outside but, according to the rules, still leaves plenty of race track width available, just none that the overtaking driver wants to use. Do this to excess these days and we might be penalised for blocking. Ultimately, the championship organisers want to see intense racing and that means overtaking!

Belgium's Circuit de Spa-Francorchamps is a fabulous track with some interesting geography, if not as extreme as the Nordschleife. The sequence from La Source down through Eau Rouge and up Raidillon can illustrate how drivers can leverage the gradients and cambers to their advantage in order to pass or defend. La Source hairpin has a helpful camber very close to the apex which, if incorporated into a tighter line, can help to slow and rotate an overtaking car more effectively than initial turn in of the normal wider racing line. You'll also see drivers using this approach in the wet, mostly to avoid the slippery rubber in the braking zone. Of course, the tighter radius means our exit can be compromised as we cannot apply full throttle with so much steering lock, so it is important to put our rival's car wide on the exit to limit their traction too. Running down the steep hill towards Eau Rouge, our adversary may still be alongside to our left as we are obliged to leave them a car's width. Their enthusiasm will wane at the bottom of the hill when they realise, despite their more optimal position over the left-hand entry kerb, our car is blocking the right-hand apex, forcing them wide on to the dirty surface up the hill. If they don't back out of it, they'll be all over the kerbs on the crest at Raidillon, compromising their speed all the way up the Kemmel straight, and these days also risking a track-limits infringement penalty.

There is so much talk these days of 'gaining an unfair advantage' if one driver or the other leaves the track during an overtake. In principle, this makes sense: you can't take a short-cut and expect to get away with it. However, with two cars tussling, often cars are forced over track limits, with one or both straight onto the radio to complain, in the hope their rival will be penalised. This is something I am very much against; I believe advantage should be gained out on the circuit, not in the stewards' office, and allowing drivers or teams to manipulate penalties for opponents is part of the reason why Formula 1 in particular has received so much criticism of late. I'll get deeper into this in the 2pm Inside Track chapter on track designs, because I consider this is often the root of the problem.

So, we've emerged from the corner, bringing in the power as soon as possible without losing traction and managing to maintain our leading position. With our compromised line and exit speed, that pesky challenger is right in our mirrors along the following straight, ready to take advantage of the hole we are punching in the air. Drafting or slipstreaming is a commonly known term where the car behind gains a speed advantage, but there are some nuances worth knowing.

Going back to 1998, Snetterton still featured the full-length old Revett Straight, a straight shot from Sear to the Esses. Our underpowered boxy Fiestas largely depended on the slipstream to maximise lap times. In my already-mentioned race-long battle with Neal Gordon, I realised the slipstream was not only to be found in the wake directly behind his car, but was also very powerful inside the 'bow-wave' next to his car. I could use this to good effect, passing Neal early in the race and then defending by allowing him alongside on Revett, grabbing that bow-wave effect as soon as he was slightly ahead and re-passing him before diving away to prevent him gaining the same advantage from my bow-wave. I think he was quite perplexed about where our extra speed was coming from, every time he thought he was past!

One event where I had to learn another new drafting technique was in the Spa 25 hours (yes, twenty-five, you read it right!). Together with the Connell family, I've contested that Fun Cup endurance race three times, with a best result in 2006, where we achieved ninth overall in a field of more than 150 supposedly identical cars from countries all over Europe. Those 'Beetle' lookalikes were not straightforward to drive with a set of hard-compound low-grip grooved tyres, a mid-engine configuration delivering a healthy 230bhp per tonne and appalling aerodynamics! The Belgians were always damn quick and they knew how to work together on track to overcome the aero drag deficiency. Pretty soon, we realised it was critical to insert our car into a train of four or five Belgians.

Cars running closely like this not only benefit from the slipstream 'tow' of the car in front, but also reduce the size (and therefore the drag) of the wake which usually slows that leading car, so the whole train can accelerate. The following cars gain still more, at Spa repeatedly bumping the cars ahead as we rocketed along the Kemmel straight! What made this 'bump drafting' even more unnerving was the central driving position in those cars, meaning the visibility past the train in front was pretty much zero. The rear windows were also opaque, thanks to the anti-glare film for the night portion of the race, so there was no view through the car either. Just like the Lotus in the rain, we had to watch for the Les Combes corner marker boards, and dive out at the last minute, making sure not to be 'connected' to the car in front or behind at that critical moment. It was not unusual to be four abreast in the braking zone! The car on the outside usually went straight on whilst the rest of us jostled through the switchbacks, sometimes still side-by-side at Malmedy.

Although drafting is also a critical tactic at the Nürburgring Nordschleife with lengthy straights, there is certainly no intentional bump drafting! At speeds in excess of 170mph (270kmh), the draft can be picked up even from a distant car and you'll frequently see passes with two wheels on the grass as drivers refuse to lift off the throttle! I've enjoyed several amusing occasions when driving mid-range cars there: a GT3 with its enormous downforce will dive through to pass us at Döttinger Höhe but thanks to the increased drag created by its wings, will run into an aerodynamic 'wall' halfway down the following straight. I've re-passed such cars with a smile and a wave, being careful to stay well out of the way as they streak past again under braking at Tiergarten! One year, we ran a wingless V12 Vantage which in qualifying along there hit a staggering 190mph (well over 300kmh); the organisers quietly asked us to back off a little in the interest of safety!

One of the most pleasurable aspects of endurance racing is the ability to compete with a huge range of different cars, each with their own strengths and weaknesses. In one-make racing, the drivers and cars up front were very equal and overtaking mainly entailed forcing a mistake from those ahead. In multi-class racing, it's more strategic, bringing an intellectual element into the game. We may have the advantage in certain sections, where we can maximise the gap to our pursuers, but their own advantages may be brought to bear later in the lap. It's incredibly satisfying to work out how to contain their attack, with minimal time loss, then exploit our car's unique capabilities to pull away again later in the lap. Over a long race stint, where tyre wear is a factor, the optimal strategy may even be to let them past, knowing that if we can preserve our rubber whilst fuel levels are high (or if there is a later safety car), we'll be in a great position on low fuel later in the stint to slipstream and re-pass them.

Also in the mix is traffic management, both ahead and behind, and the use of those cars to delay our opponents. Lapping slower cars is a matter of anticipation as already described, ideally timing the pass to minimise speed loss. However, we don't have that luxury in the cut-and-thrust of battle. Timing of the pass is then more about making sure the position of the lapped car forces the greatest compromise to the line of the aggressor on our rear bumper. If we can dive through just in time to access the full track width on the corner exit, we can gain a key advantage and maybe break the tow. More complex is dealing with faster classes coming up behind to lap us; simultaneously, we need to repel the challenge of competitors in our own class, who will try to 'hang you out to dry' by following the quicker cars through a corner. The best tactical option depends on the specific track configuration and whether the tow from the faster car will be a critical element in the following section. Generally, I will rely on the later braking capability of a faster class car, and make sure I can cut back to the apex behind it, always checking they are not part of their own multi-car train!

Nürburgring 24 hours races are unusual in that they use the very smooth Formula 1 Grand Prix track with its gravel-traps and low kerbs, in combination with the much narrower, bumpier, twistier Nordschleife to create two quite different ordeals over a single lap. Cars that are super-quick in one part are often slow in the next, a factor that needs to be considered to avoid being delayed later in the lap. Often, less-experienced drivers will give me hell around the Grand

Prix track section, lunging here and there in the braking zones, more experienced and confident on that surface, only to fall away as we plunge down into the Nordschleife through Hatzenbach, their tyres likely overheated from their earlier over-enthusiasm. If I let them through on the GP circuit, they'll be even slower on the Nordschleife with me filling their mirrors.

With so many cars and many hundreds of drivers competing on a track with a huge variety of features, Nürburgring 24 hours races are endlessly fascinating events which for me encapsulate the complete race-craft challenge and opportunity for the most committed race car drivers in the world. It's why I keep going back...

PEOPLE POWER

A motor racing team is quite distinct from teams in other sports such as football, rugby, basketball, ice-hockey and the like. Those sports feature a relatively large number of very visible, often-interchangeable players, who carry to a large degree the responsibility, and rightly the recognition, for their team's success in the face of competition.

In almost all motorsport teams of any size, there is evidently a huge imbalance. The racing drivers are also highly-visible and every podium has three of them spraying champagne and brandishing their trophy spoils of war. However, their success is disproportionately dependent on the work of many others, including the designers, engineers and fabricators inside and outside the factory, the mechanics in the pit garage and the race engineers and strategists on the pit wall. Aside from a few individual opportunities to stand next to the driver podium, rarely do these folks gain the recognition proportional to the extent of their influence. If this team has done their job to the absolute maximum, we might even say only the driver can be responsible for losing the race!

I appreciate this point will ruffle a few feathers amongst the driver community, particularly those who are precious about protecting their careers, but how much of a competitive difference can they really make on track if the team behind them is not functional or supportive? People power is everything. It's the reason why on the podium, contrived as it may seem, we often hear the winning driver exclaim, "The team has done a fantastic job back at the factory!" It's an acknowledgement that has become a cliché, but nevertheless has far more depth than is perhaps apparent.

The relationship a driver has with the team is paramount. Given the tiny fractions between success and second place, even small differences in motivation hidden somewhere in the team hierarchy will be magnified on track. Perhaps somewhere right now, there are two Formula 3 teams preparing cars for their equally talented and ambitious young drivers. The FIA has defined the gear ratios to be used for the next race and the mechanics are assembling their respective gearboxes accordingly. Come race week, one of those teams runs a slightly higher top-speed than the other, despite the same aero settings. Somebody somewhere deep in the quicker team stayed late in the workshop, maybe even accompanied by their driver, taking more care with the gearbox assembly tolerances, minimising frictional losses and ensuring maximum power delivery and vital tenths over a lap. The other team removes wing to recover the top speed difference and their driver wonders why the hell they still can't match that lap time.

In my own three decades and more racing, I've spent as much time as possible with the team's engineers and mechanics, limited only by the fact that for much of my driving career, I had in parallel a full-time job with Dow Automotive, also one of my sponsors. I'll help where possible, although in such a professional environment, it's a little like the ambulance driver trying to help the surgeons! I can use my background in automotive engineering and design to at least speak their language and bring constructive ideas and solutions to the table. I'm keen to review the telemetry and take advice on possible driving technique improvements, something which brings a powerful sense of shared ownership and recognition within the team when the results come. I'm proud of our achievements together and my trophies almost always stay with the team.

When things go wrong, I'll not bullshit anyone, as I know trust between driver and team is critical. I want them to know their extra efforts to get the car back to perfect won't be wasted. I've brought crates of beer to the track for the mechanics when I have damaged the car. That cuts two ways: if we have endured a strategic or mechanical failure, I expect honesty in return, allowing me to maintain the confidence I need in the team and the car. Sometimes this pushes tensions to the extreme, for example after that high-speed 2016 crash at Kesselchen. It took a lot of patient dialogue with the team boss (the patience was on his side) for me to be satisfied it really was down to driver error and not a suspension or tyre failure. Without the very solid carefully-built relationship with Aston Martin, such a crash could easily have been my last outing with that team.

The relationship with driver team mates is also something that can hinder progress if not nurtured and maintained. Unlike endurance racing, sprint racing team mates are rarely both competitive and supportive. Slower team mates are always keen to work together but are unable to help in terms of set-up input or on-track tactics. Faster team mates tend to either keep things to themselves, like my 2001 BTCC partner James Kaye, or try to spin you a yarn to obscure how they are really finding their speed.

It's of course not unusual for the faster driver to receive more attention and access to better equipment. Despite the intent for contractual parity between cars, the team will place their bets on the most likely winner if there is a choice to be made. In the 2001 BTCC round at Oulton Park, I recall having to continue with somewhat basic two-way dampers, whilst team stalwart James enjoyed the single set of new four-way equivalents, allowing him much more aggressive kerb use. I was forced to experiment with some interesting kerb-straddling lines in an attempt to compensate for this disadvantage!

Tough times always test the mettle of every team and they all, including the drivers, have different ways of dealing with it. At Oulton Park two years prior, our Vectra team suffered a terrible result with all three cars. All I can recall is some bar very late at night, in Northwich I think, and rather more Drambuie than can be healthy! At that low moment, we kind of forgot the fact we were due to travel up to Scotland the next day to test at Knockhill before the next race there, and that certainly wasn't my finest performance behind the wheel. Knockhill is a fantastic track, with some incredible elevation changes through Duffus Dip or especially the chicane where we launch the car over the left-hand kerb and literally take off over the crest and the right-hand kerb, landing on the far side still just about on track if we've done it right. It's just not a circuit to drive with a raging hangover, even if the poor condition of my head taught me to find the absolutely smoothest lines on that test day! I should point out at this stage that I've always been crap at dealing with alcohol, as all my close friends well know. I suspect it was because I was teetotal for a number of years, when I was really trying to find every opportunity to maximise my racing performance. For whatever reason, it still takes relatively little beer, wine or the hard stuff to turn me into a giggling inappropriate joke machine.

Although I've always tried to treat others as I'd like to be treated, things weren't always rosy with my team mates. Barwell Motorsport ran two other Vectras that year. James was new to Vectras like me, a very easy-going funny guy, a natural racer who had done well in MGFs winning from the front, but I considered him less effective in traffic. Jason was different, more focused and aggressive which I could respect, especially as this was his third year in the championship and his career needed a good result. We had a bit of an issue at Donington, where we had agreed to run in whatever order resulted after the start, so we could focus on beating the other teams. That lasted until Jason threw his car up the inside of mine at Redgate! As the motorsport ladder is climbed, the competitive tension is ratcheted up and I realised there was little room for generosity or teamsmanship even at that level.

Barwell Motorsport Team Principal Mark Lemmer's competitive nature sometimes got the better of him in those days, especially if he thought the driver was not following instructions, as happened at a

Brands Hatch Vectra test. The Dunlop tyres we used were only good for a couple of qualifying laps, and in the race we had to manage them carefully to make them last. Why championships do this is beyond me: spectators want to see racers drive flat out every lap and racers want to drive flat out every lap. Even Formula 1 has fallen into this trap; it is to the detriment of the sport and forces other artificial measures to spice up the show. Anyway, towards the end of that test day, I was on the old Dunlops and keen to see how they lasted, so I ran several more laps than planned. I caught the raw end of Mark's wrath, even before I got out of the car! I kept my helmet visor down, but it still left a bitter taste in my mouth. More than anyone, I wanted to perform well and impress the boss. I suffered a more public reprimand later at Oulton Park after Mat Jackson and Tom Boardman had savaged our Accord. Many onlookers incorrectly thought that Mark's anger was the reason for me leaving the team, but it was always short-lived. I understood it was just an expression of his desire to achieve the best possible result and to grow what has since become a hugely successful top-level international GT race team. I'd much rather work with that kind of direct, undisguised emotion than some of the snakes I've encountered in the paddock.

By far the most toxic team environment I encountered was at Team B&Q Jet York City in 2002. In my opinion, 'Junior', the driver of the team's sister car, turned out to be the worst 'team mate' I ever had: he adopted an unwelcoming, uncommunicative and generally unhelpful approach which was allowed to persist by the weak team management. This whole sorry episode serves to show I did not have the support of the team when it mattered. I had perceived that the power rested with team owner John Batchelor and had concentrated on building a relationship with him, with the expectation he would override any resistance I encountered from Junior or team manager Stuart. In June, I could see we were headed for conflict and wrote a lengthy letter to John about Junior's conduct at the time. Here's a short excerpt:

> *I think it would be fantastic if we can sort things out so that it is clear to him that the drivers in this team are equal in status. I believe that he still sees me as the new arrival, an unnecessary hindrance to his championship on track and of course he does not like to be beaten. The fact is, you want the best drivers who can also provide the best service to your sponsors and fans. That is what I am striving to be and I hope that shows sufficiently to overcome any 'people issues' we might face. I don't think there needs to be any problem with him and I am keen to make this work but I need your help to get him to that point.*

Unfortunately for me, John elected to leave matters in the hands of Stuart. Despite the impressive results we achieved together, running at the front and even securing podiums as a brand-new team, on 4th July, I received a formal letter from Stuart, essentially ending my contract with the team for reasons that were entirely fabricated on his part. As I filed many documents over the years, I am able quote that letter word-for-word here below:

Dear Peter

After careful consideration of the needs of the team, I have concluded that it is in the best interest of everybody concerned that you are no longer a part of it. Your presence at Croft is therefore not required as a driver or in any other capacity.

Our official reason for TOCA will be that due to general work pressure and increasing family commitments you have decided that you are no longer able to give the necessary commitment to the team for the rest of the season.

Your acceptance of the general principal of this statement will be best for all concerned and will maintain your future prospects in motor racing in the best and most positive light.

May I take this opportunity of thanking you for your input this far, some of which has taken the team forward. I wish you well for the future.

Yours faithfully,
Stuart

What motivated Stuart to take this action? With hindsight, I believe he needed to protect Junior, who brought that 1999 car to the team in exchange for driving the 2001 specification car and who doubtless was understandably unhappy to be beaten on numerous occasions by his old specification car. Apparently it wasn't the first time I'd embarrassed Junior: back in 2000, after I successfully tested a Mark

Fish Clio at Silverstone, I recall he threatened to leave that team if I was allowed to race, because he felt that I had made him look foolish in front of TOCA. Consequently, after discussion with Mark, I stood down and did not race. Yet Junior was a proven quick driver and Clio Cup champion. Puzzling as it seems, I guess by dealing with a challenge to his success off track, rather than on it, he was compensating for a lack of confidence in his abilities behind the wheel.

After I left, Junior's new team mate was the rapid Hyla Breese, who that season endured seven DNS (did not start) and a DNF, his only finishes being 9th and 11th (both at Snetterton). Hyla suffered so many engine changes, the resulting penalties meant he became the first BTCC driver in the championship's history to end the championship on negative points. I was not surprised. You'd be right to say, after the initial disappointment, I was relieved to be out of that toxic team environment. Maybe that 4th July was my Independence Day!

Another significant paddock character I believe I misjudged, was TOCA Fiesta team-owner and aging racer Colin Stancombe, whose team I drove with in 1997. Directly after my first Fiesta race, I was basking in the glory of a second-place finish at Donington when Colin came up to me in *parc fermé*. Instead of offering the congratulations you'd expect of your new team owner and team mate (he drove a Fiesta in the championship too), he snarled in front of everybody there, "You won't find it so easy next time!" He was right and I had no idea why at the time. Clearly it was within his power to increase or decrease the performance of the cars in his charge and I guess he felt I did not deserve the optimal package any longer. In searching for an explanation, I think it might have been something to do with the first meeting we had the previous season at Oulton Park, before I had signed to drive with him: I'd asked him why his cars weren't winning and perhaps he decided to show me.

I do recall he was furious sometime mid-season after I wrote him a cheque that bounced (actually because I had dropped my cheque book in a chippy in Maldon, and the bank stopped all the uncashed cheques when it was handed in). Colin handled it really badly, accusing me of spending 'Daddy's money'. For the record, he was 100% wrong, as you'll know from the 5pm On The Road chapter! The relationship went from bad to worse after he repeatedly drove into my car down the Craner Curves during our second visit to Donington that season, grinning across at me like a maniac as he earned himself damage repairs each time we touched.

My last recollection of Colin was at Oulton Park when I rolled the Barwell Motorsport Vectra during testing at the end of 1998. Although I had left his Fiesta team the previous year, he still saw fit to rush over to the Barwell crew in the pit lane and vociferously claim the crash was all my fault. Still trying to screw me, all that time later... Chris Needell, Commercial Director at Barwell stood firm and didn't allow Colin's pettiness to influence their decision to sign me for 1999 and beyond. All this was great learning for me: surround yourself with trustworthy and talented people, develop and leave behind good relationships at all levels and recognise the motor racing paddock is small: your paths will almost certainly cross again!

Even though I was forced to leave Barwell in 2001, crushing my BTCC dreams, I remained good friends with Mark, Chris and the team. Barwell repaid that friendship when Aston Martin's Head of Motorsport approached them requesting a reference for me in 2009. It was a great pleasure 16 years later to be reunited with Mark and James Kaye as we shared an Audi TCR at a typically soaking Spa 12 hours. It was like flicking a switch back on: everything operated just as it did all those years ago!

DIRTY TRICKS?

Contestants of all sports have long recognised the advantages to be gained by destabilising their opponents. The world-famous New Zealand rugby team's war haka is performed to intimidate the 'enemy' (as well as strengthen unity within the team) and is a very public, entirely accepted psychological component of the competition.

In my experience, there are many other less visible practices with the same ultimate goal to disadvantage and weaken rivals, both on and off the track. In 1987, Nelson Piquet allegedly removed all the toilet paper from the pit garage after noticing Williams Formula 1 team mate Nigel Mansell was suffering the after-effects of the local Mexican cuisine. Amusing as this tale is, the implications for Nigel could have been pretty serious, particularly under heavy braking!

Racing of course is fuelled by a desire to compete, to prove ourselves against competition, to win. The ambiguity comes with the question, to win but at what cost? Nelson's prank is probably acceptable to some degree but what if he had gone further, slipping laxatives into Nigel's breakfast coffee? Where is the line? Most of us know the answer instinctively, but the heat of battle distorts the picture to the extent that for some, in the words of Joey Tribbiani, "The line is a dot to you!"

Someone crossed that line in the early 1990s, when we qualified on pole at Brands Hatch with the Litchfield Class B Alfasud. Typical of club racing, our car was left overnight in the paddock on an open trailer whilst Dad and I slept in a local B&B. The next morning, we started up the engine, drove it slowly through the tunnel to the collecting area, then out onto the grid. All was well on the formation lap, my focus on warming up the massive slicks and brakes. It was only as the start line gantry's red lights came on and the revs rose that I realised we had something of a misfire.

As I dumped the clutch and set off up to the awesome Paddock Hill Bend, the engine sputtered and the car just would not accelerate beyond a crawl. I hugged the apex kerb tightly, expecting the crunch of glass-fibre from the rear at any second. Fortunately, I pulled over at the bottom of Hailwood's Hill unscathed but furious. How could the car be misbehaving, untouched, after performing so well the previous day? It transpired that it had not been untouched. Our checks afterwards revealed that the spade connector that powered the main electric fuel pump was no longer attached, despite it being well protected under the car. Running only on the smaller pump, the car had shown no symptoms at low speed but completely choked with full throttle demand off the start line. Had the fuel pump been sabotaged by someone with a grievance and enough knowledge to facilitate this dirty trick? Almost certainly. The outcome was a lost point scoring opportunity, a wasted journey, a lot of cost and very luckily no damage or injuries.

Sabotage is a strong accusation to make. My dad is Dutch-born and Holland is of course a country famous for its clogs. The irony of that was lost on me until recently, when I learned the word 'sabotage' in fact comes from the old French 'sabot', the name for a wooden clog favoured by 19th century textile workers. With the arrival of the Jacquard looms that they saw were replacing their jobs, 'saboteurs' would throw their sabots into the loom machinery with the intention to wreck them! Had there been any such footwear lying around at Brands Hatch that day, it may well have been thrown! Thankfully the fuel pump mystery seemed to be an isolated incident, and as far as I know, my race cars were not obviously sabotaged throughout the rest of the 1990s.

My Autobytel Lotus Championship experience in 2000 however, was a cautionary tale. So many things went wrong, I began to suspect either gross incompetence on the part of the mechanics or worse, foul play. The first suspicious moment was early in the season at Thruxton where we qualified fifth in baking temperatures, just 0.3 seconds from pole. Lotus had to enlarge the slots in the engine bay cover to help manage the heat. I was looking forward to a close race, but incredibly the car dropped all its coolant in the collecting area, leaving me to trudge over to the hospitality unit to explain to sponsors Anadin Ultra that the car would not be running. It turned out the Jubilee clip on the coolant hose had been loosened and not tightened up. Why anyone would have needed to interfere with this between qualifying and the race was beyond me, but those oversize engine cover slots gave easy access to the clip for anyone with bad intentions and a screwdriver.

Two races later we were at Silverstone. I'd qualified second on the grid behind eventual championship winner Adam Wilcox. As the cars joined the track for the race on Sunday to complete their warming up lap, I noticed something was amiss with the rev counter. I was trying to get some heat into the tyres as usual, but noticed that as I accelerated along the straight, the revs were rising too rapidly and reading far too high for the gear and speed. Quick checks on the grid could not correct the problem and I was forced to start 'blind', with no way of knowing how high the engine was actually revving other than by ear.

At the start, as usual I held it around 6000rpm on the dash as the red lights came on, concerned not to over-rev it, but clearly the revs were actually much lower in reality, as the engine just bogged down as the lights went green. I learned afterwards that the tacho was reading about 150% too high. I spoke with the specialist engineers from Stack (the telemetry system suppliers), and they confirmed it had been tampered with, basically reset to read a three-cylinder engine. This was only possible with a complex set of very intentional multi-button inputs. Consequently, the Anadin car was slow off the line and several cars simply drove past me around the first lap. It took me a couple of laps to work out how inaccurate the tacho was, using the usual track references for the gear shift points. I ended up having to change gear off the dial!

The Elises were all prepared by the Lotus mechanics, within large paddock tents which each housed five cars. Coincidentally, my car was in the same tent as Adam's. No driver was allowed to bring their own mechanics, but out of hours access to the Lotus tent would have been a simple matter and I began to wonder if I should spend a night in the tent with a camera to ensure nothing was amiss in the morning.

At every one of the next three races, something untoward happened to my car, increasing suspicions that sabotage was the source of my problems. At Croft, the car suffered cooling problems again. At Snetterton, I was forced to pull over when the low battery warning light came on and the engine died. At Donington, my throttle cable let go, just beneath the pedal. Was it paranoia to suspect outside meddling after experiencing so many race-stopping incidents? Certainly, finding my suspension was misaligned in the Donington practice session didn't alleviate my misgivings.

Things became much more serious on our second visit to Silverstone, a second night race. Before qualifying, there was a night-time familiarisation session for the drivers, especially to allow them to get used to the way the circuit was floodlit in the grandstand areas. As the cars assembled in the collecting area, I noticed a curl of smoke in the cockpit of our car. I slipped off the belts and got out. When I looked back at the car, it was like looking into an erupting volcano crater! The entire engine bay was ablaze, with flames leaping into the sky, and it took the concerted effort of several marshals to extinguish the fire. It turned out that the oil filter was not properly tightened and sealed in place, allowing oil to spray onto the hot exhaust manifold and explode into flame. Once again, this was a component easily accessible within the engine bay. #17 would not run that night, the Lotus team working late to clean up the mess left by the fire extinguishers, and to check for fire damage. The implications of this disaster occurring out on track were potentially life-threatening, especially if the oil spray had pitched me into the barrier prior to the fire.

Shortly after, we travelled over to Magny-Cours in October for the last race of that season. In qualifying, entering Estoril corner at over 100mph, the rear end let go instantaneously, pitching the car into a looping spin. I could feel something was amiss at the rear. I could also see that the water temperature had suddenly shot up so I just took it easy back to the pits and let the guys check it out. It transpired that the engine coolant hose had once again come away due to a loose clip, spraying coolant all over the rear tyres and causing the car to slide. If someone was sabotaging our car, you'd have thought they would apply a bit more imagination to come up with some new tricks.

That appalling year 2000 with Lotus heightened my level of involvement with car preparation, checking what I could, probably to the frustration of the mechanics. I need not have worried in 2001: the Barwell Honda was impeccably prepared and the only issues I experienced were in the cut-and-thrust of on-track competition. However, in 2002 with Team B&Q Jet York City I was plunged right back into the dark world of suspicion and mistrust.

Thruxton in June was my first race with this BTCC team and as you've read earlier, I qualified ahead of my team mate Junior for both races. I wasn't actually at all happy in qualifying; the balance of the car from practice was gone. It turned out the smaller offset rear wheels had been fitted to the front and vice versa, causing a lot of understeer. Was this very poor attention to preparation or sabotage? Switching the wheels back to their correct locations allowed me to run at the front in both the Sprint race and later in the feature race, until an oil leak pitched the car off the track at the high-speed Noble left-hander.

We intended to start the next race at Silverstone with a similar set-up from Thruxton. Arriving on Saturday, I could see the car just looked wrong. We checked and found it had mysteriously risen around 20mm in ride height all around, even though I was assured it had not been changed by the team. With the car up on stands, increasing ride height is a quick adjustment to the spring platforms but as I've mentioned, not only will it negatively affect the car's centre of gravity, it also has a significant influence upon corner-weights and handling. It's a crude but effective method to slow a car down. The team dropped it down again to approximately the correct ride heights before qualifying but as expected, the handling was all messed up. When we later put the car on the corner-weight scales, they were naturally way off the settings from Thruxton. Being hit at Copse by Junior in the feature race was the icing on the sarcasm cake that weekend.

Things became even darker at Mondello, my last races with the team. In the Sprint race, running in second place off the start and looking to attack the leading BMW of Norman Simon, I felt something was not right at Lola corner and braked slightly early for the double right at Tarzan. My brake pedal went to the floor! I kept it out of the wall thanks to the gravel trap and crept back into the pits, the pedal recovering pressure as the system cooled. Suspecting that there was air in the brake system or that the brake fluid had boiled (something which should not have happened if racing brake fluid was used), I insisted it was changed for the feature race. I approached my old team Barwell who kindly supplied replacement fluid and despite team boss Stuart telling me to take it easy on the brakes, I was competitive again, shadowing Junior home to a double-podium result. A few weeks later I received the fateful letter forcing my departure. I guess they had run out of ideas to manage the competitive situation between Junior and I.

Even if there were reasonable grounds for inquiry, I cannot say for certain that all these occurrences I experienced were sabotage: I will leave that to conjecture. I do know for certain that my enjoyment of racing was compromised to the extent that I'd had enough anyway. Competitive pressure is one thing, but with Kim and I having married in 2001 and with our first daughter on the way in 2002, the idea that someone might be prepared to sabotage my car to the extent that I could be injured or killed was not a risk I was prepared to take.

On a lighter note, many years later with Aston Martin, I managed to sabotage myself! On such a long lap as the Nordschleife, with many radio dead-spots, we typically carry a mobile phone in the car for emergencies. That year, we used our own phones, mine being tucked into the leg pocket of my race suit. The car was running well, except every time I came down the start-finish straight, the engine would cut out! It would fire up again around the Yokohama S but then cut again on the run up to the NGK Schikane. We only realised later that my phone was still switched on and it was attempting to connect with the pit-suite Wi-Fi as I drove past, somehow interfering with the race car's specialist steering-wheel electronics. Needless to say, switching off my phone has since become a double-check in my pre-stint protocol!

KEEPING THE FAITH

In the wilderness of late 2002, a friend Paul Taylor reached out and asked if I was available to share a car with him in a one-hour endurance race at Silverstone. As I had my race licence, kit and more spare time than expected, I agreed, not really understanding what I was signing up to.

The race car was a 2CV, one of 29 starters that cold November day, each supposedly developing a whopping 40bhp! Qualifying conditions were damp and slippery; I had never been so sideways so often and for so long in a front-wheel-drive car! I had to shut out much of what I knew from previous racing, the priority being to keep the momentum going and the throttle hard down. We only finished eighth, knowing our engine probably needed an overhaul after guys we'd just lapped would drive past again on the following straight. Nevertheless, as I said at the time, I never realised I could have so much fun going so slowly. With hindsight, I can see this race with Paul was a spark that helped reignite my passion for racing.

Over the winter, Brunswick Racing, run by Giles Groombridge, reached out with an opportunity to do some endurance racing in the EERC (European Endurance Racing Club) and British GT Championship with their own Lotus, funded by gentleman co-driver Rachid. After a random encounter with 'Mr Bean' in the pit garage (Rowan was in fact looking for the Clerk of the Course), we qualified on class pole in the first race at Donington, bringing me a much-needed boost. I began to enjoy the process of helping Rachid get up to speed and there was no fear of sabotage: everyone was pulling together.

The same team also took me back to Spa for the 1000km, sharing the seat this time with two other like-minded drivers. Yes, of course it rained! At the British GT Championship Oulton Park round, I had the privilege to share their Lotus with ex-Formula 1 driver and world sportscar champion Vincenzo Sospiri. I learned some useful techniques from that super-quick guy. Try for example exhaling before you hit the brakes on the approach to a corner you find particularly daunting: you will be so much more relaxed and smoother with the controls.

These events with Brunswick cemented my growing belief that endurance racing was the way to recover my passion for racing, even if things didn't always go our way on track. At Oulton for example, I was punted off into the gravel trap when that previously mentioned Lotus driver with the erroneous indicator habit hit a Golf at the Knickerbrook chicane, the Golf then smashing into the rear of our Lotus, breaking the right rear wheel rim.

My difficulties especially with the Elise in 2000 had taught me an inner resolve which I later realised is a very necessary characteristic for any racer: what doesn't kill you makes you stronger (except for bears, as Canadians will tell you: they just kill you!). Let's leave aside the seven or eight issues mentioned in the previous chapter which may or may not have been down to sabotage. During only the first weekend of the 2000 Autobytel Lotus Championship season at Brands Hatch, I experienced a right-rear tyre exploding at Surtees, a qualifying crash at Dingle Dell (the awesome jump configuration) trying to avoid a spun Paula Cook and finally that race-ending heavy crash at Westfield.

It's tough to pick yourself up from that, only to be confronted by a mechanical failure at the next race, stuck in fifth gear after battling for third-place at Donington. The gear selector or linkage then failed again later in the season at Silverstone in practice and at the Brands Hatch double-header in qualifying and in both races. At Oulton Park, an exhaust bracket broke, robbing the car of crucial top speed. Perhaps I would have endured that failure at the previous Thruxton race had I even been able to get out of the collecting area. The same exhaust fault then occurred at Donington, where in addition, the gearbox casing came away from the engine, spraying gearbox lubricant all over my rear tyres, leading to a shunt up the rear as the car behind struggled to slow on my spilled oil. A driveshaft failed at Croft leading to a split gaiter which sprayed grease over my rear tyres, the oversteer eventually running me just wide enough to catch a marker board which holed the radiator. Even without any fluid leak, another smash up the rear destroyed our race car at the Nürburgring.

I know I am amongst the many drivers who have endured appalling seasons, even whose careers have been ended by seasons less disappointing than this, their teams losing faith (or money) and sponsors walking away. It comes down to keeping alive a flame of determination, in my case fuelled by a strong sense of injustice, and using that to illuminate new pathways back into a driving seat which can be found even in the most unexpected places.

Whilst I had been driving their Lotus, Brunswick had also been running an Alfa Romeo 156 in the EERC races, piloted by Dave Ashford and Dave Smith (of mid-1980s England cricket team fame). Giles convinced me to join them in that car for the 2003 Nürburgring 24 hours race in the A3 class, along with ex-Alfa Romeo Championship racer Gary Lucas. Even though I'd visited the Nürburgring to race the Grand Prix track in 2000, I had no idea how to tackle the hills and valleys of its much less civilised big brother, the Nordschleife. A few weeks prior, I hired a Toyota Verso from Europcar (not my specific car of choice!) and, this being pre-YouTube era, strapped an old camcorder onto the dashboard to get a rudimentary sense of which way the track went over those crests and around those blind corners! Watching that video at home every night was a huge benefit, as it was effectively slow-motion in that car; on the climb from Bergwerk, I actually had to change down a gear to maintain speed, such was the gradient!

It's worth relaying a few years later at Zurich airport, I arrived at the Europcar desk late at night and they said, "We cannot rent you a car!" I presented my reservation and began to complain when they cut me short: "You have been racing in one of our cars." After a brief show of feigned ignorance, I tried to argue I had simply taken a gentle tour of the Nordschleife in their Audi A4 with my friend and that it is in fact a public toll road. This was true: any road vehicle capable of more than 60kmh (in those days), even a bus, was entitled to buy a ticket and drive a lap on a 'Touristenfahrt' day. They replied, "In that case, why were you both wearing helmets?" I had been giving some instruction to my Norwegian racing friend Lars (who since became an instructor himself at Sport Driving GmbH), and it turned out there was a photographer at the track entry barrier who could recognise rental cars. His photo was in my Europcar file, along with an apparent lifetime rental ban. Fortunately, there are other rental car companies available!

Back to that first Nürburgring 24 hours race in 2003, a cheap flight from Stansted to Frankfurt-Hahn, an hour's drive or so through the beautiful and entertaining Bernkastel-Wittlich district roads and I was there in the paddock for what would become the focus of my racing life for the next two decades and more.

Things began in a manner typical of the Green Hell. During the qualifying day, the skies darkened and an immense thunderstorm literally flooded the track in the evening. This delayed the start of the second qualifying session when I was due to run my mandatory two laps. By the time the session started an hour late at 8pm, everyone was keen to get out there on what was a very tricky half-wet half-dry track!

As I've mentioned, this race is contested on a combination of the Grand Prix track (where the pit lane is located) and the Nordschleife. I left the pits and brought the car around the GP circuit to the point where drivers can turn right and cut through to the start-finish straight, in order to start a full lap without having to drive around the entire 13-mile (20.8km) Nordschleife circuit. As I approached, a Porsche 996 dived up the right-hand side as if to turn right into the cut-through ahead of us, before apparently changing his mind and continuing straight on. Despite taking avoiding action, I couldn't avoid being swiped by the rear corner of the 996, which immediately punctured the front right tyre, damaged the suspension and forced a change to a more standard gearbox which meant we'd have to race without a limited-slip differential.

The further concern was that I had not completed my two qualifying laps and perhaps would not be allowed to take the start of the race. The team worked frantically to strip the gearbox, but it became obvious that despite a fantastic team effort, the curtailed qualifying session would not give them enough time to get the car out again. Fortunately, after later reviewing the situation, the very understanding Clerk of the Course decided to allow me to drive in the race, despite my inexperience there, dispelling my ignorant preconceptions about Germans being sticklers for rule following! In fact, over the years, I have seen things at the Nordschleife that would make UK track officials' toes curl. Taking a bit of a track walk late evening that year, we heard something approaching and a helmetless maniac zipped by at the wheel of a racing go-kart. Nobody seemed to mind. Just try that at Silverstone before the fluorescent jackets appear!

At three o'clock on Saturday 31st May, I took my first Nürburgring 24 hours race start, one of 230 cars on track! I had never experienced anything like the warm-up lap. It seemed like most of the hundreds of thousands of fans were literally on the track, particularly crowded between the Armco through the Hatzenbach and up the hill to the Karussell. They all wanted to high-five the drivers and touch the cars.

We were going so slowly I was worried the engine would overheat! When we all piled through those sections a lap later in the race proper, I expected to see a few stragglers, but they were all back in the spectator areas, flags waving and airhorns blasting.

The fans at the Nordschleife are amazing, seemingly a different breed. Not only do they appear at the 24 hour race more than a week before, but they'll build impossible scaffolding-based constructions with sofas atop, to gain a better view over the fence. Their camps are enormous, filled with bonfires or braziers, rock music blaring, with a seemingly endless supply of fireworks and flares in their old VW buses or caravans. What is even more impressive, on a Monday evening after the race you'd hardly know they were ever there, all the litter neatly packed into bins and nothing of their encampments left behind. Not quite like Glastonbury...

I managed to avoid the first lap chaos and aside from an oil pressure issue during Gary's stint, we motored into the night, the car running quicker as temperatures dropped. Campfire smoke, some dewy morning mist, an eyes-wide moment for me thanks to oil on track at Adenauer-Forst and an altercation for Giles with an aggressive Saab 93 Turbo brought us within sight of the finish. Even a failing CV joint couldn't stop us: this was packed with grease and, to the cheering of the crowd as each car crossed the line, we completed 99 laps of the Green Hell to take the chequered flag! To put this into perspective, the winner of the top class, the Team Phoenix Opel Astra V8 Coupe, completed 143 laps, but we didn't care! There is a huge release of emotion at the end of a 24 hour race, whether caused by lack of sleep or too many energy drinks. For the photoshoot afterwards, Gary wore a T-shirt with a picture of a fish and a single very appropriate word on it: 'Battered!'

I was still elated when I arrived home, not just with our achievement but because I'd seen the future of my racing. Sure, I would still contest other races at different tracks but I already knew the Nordschleife had me hooked. In the following years, alongside various drives at UK tracks and at Spa, I raced many different privateer cars at the 'Ring, building up my knowledge and experiencing the many highs and lows that come with the territory.

I shared a Renault Clio Sport in 2004 with the quick and far too witty Chris Harris, although this was back when he had more hair on his head than on his face! Chris wrote a very insightful article about our race in Autocar (the car's primary sponsor), especially highlighting the mental challenge of returning to the track after one of our other team mates had suffered a heavy shunt at Pflanzgarten.

In 2005, Brunswick contacted me about driving their beautiful red-and-white Mazda RX7 in the Silverstone Britcar 24 hours. This was certainly a quite different lesson in keeping the faith! The team had fitted a new rotary engine for the event but in practice and qualifying, it was not pulling properly and misfiring all through the rev range. Carl of Hayward Rotary actually built a replacement overnight back in Newbury and the team fitted it in the small hours of the morning, amidst flooded pit garages, thanks to a tremendous thunderstorm and downpour over the circuit. At the start, with the rain unabated, it was clear the engine was still malfunctioning at anything more than light throttle. I had to pull in, the first of 31 pit stops, to allow the team to investigate.

I was in awe of the Brunswick mechanics. Despite already having had little sleep the previous night, they just never gave up and tried every possibility to correct the problem, even after the car stopped out on the circuit in the middle of the night. I have never seen a team work so hard and that includes the refuelling team who were there on cue throughout, despite the numerous stops. With Carl attempting to override the misfire with engine map changes, the Mazda made an impressive sight, hammering past the pit wall in the darkness, with a metre-long blue flame from the exhaust! It was eventually clear that only half the rotary engine was functioning as it should, and the problem was eventually traced to the specialist injectors used. Replacing these meant yet another trip to the workshop for Carl, who by this time was well up in the competition for no sleep.

Eventually, in broad daylight with five hours to go, I took the car out of the pit lane once more, having been used to the lack of power: the wheelspin almost stuck me in the wall! It was clear that the problem was solved and the car immediately proceeded to set competitive times, around four seconds faster than any car in our class, on a damp and greasy track. The funniest moment occurred when Kelvin Burt, driving the leading Porsche, came up behind me before Maggotts. I let him past under blue flags, being many laps in arrears, danced the brake-throttle shuffle through Becketts and then on the Hangar Straight with the engine working perfectly, I simply drove right past him again with a shrug! It goes to show what we might have achieved with that RX7. We took the flag at five o'clock, to the delight not only of the team but also apparently many TV viewers and radio listeners worldwide who had been emailing and texting in their support of the Mazda, having witnessed the incredible efforts of Brunswick Racing!

Back at the Nürburgring, a carbon-fibre black Yale-backed lightweight Honda Civic Type R would be my ride in 2005 and 2006, with Peter Venn, Marcel Hoppe and the much-missed Dave Allan. The highlight was a 22nd-place overall finish, despite falling to the very back of around 200 starters in the first hour after a back-marker pushed Dave into the barrier. We literally drove it like we stole it and it never missed a beat, despite the hail and snow on track. We even unlapped ourselves, passing the A3-class-winning BMW 320i! 2006 didn't yield the same outcome: Nürburgring specialist Kai Riemer joined our crew but a loss of second gear and exhaust fumes leaking into the cockpit set us back mid-race. I then got caught out by a pile-up at Brünnchen, being surprised to find a spun Seat and a hard-braking BMW just around that blind corner. The resulting damage to our specialist radiator looked minor but sadly ended our race.

In 2007 and 2008, I switched to the German Schumann Motorsport team from Saarbrücken, driving their Hyundai Coupe. In those days, I'd sleep wherever I could find a cheap B&B, sometimes 20 or 30 minutes away from the track. Returning according to our driver schedule on that occasion, I parked up in the very early hours of the morning and walked over the bridge into the paddock, only to suddenly realise I could hear no race engines! It turned out the officials had quite rightly called a temporary halt to the race, as visibility was dangerously low due to fog. When the race was finally restarted, Christian Hohenadel, Adi Schumann, Peter Schumann and I pushed hard, achieving a result of 13th overall and winning the SP4 class, my first 24 hour race victory. Interestingly, I heard that the Hyundai big cheeses in Korea learned of our performance and called Schumann afterwards to make enquiries about future involvement. As a result, for quite a few years afterwards, Schumann ran a Hyundai i30 at the 'Ring and I understand the heritage of the now-famous Hyundai N brand can be traced back to our 2007 Nürburgring success!

However, 2008 with Schumann could not have been more different. First, Peter Schumann was caught up in an accident with a Porsche and a Renault at the tricky Metzgesfeld left-hander, which damaged the Hyundai's steering and rear suspension. Then during our recovery drive (from 226th position), the gearbox stuck in fourth gear necessitating yet another pit-stop. There were still 15 hours to go when I had a one of those telephone calls around midnight, when you know something is wrong before you even answer. It was the chief engineer telling me that Adi had been involved in a crash and whilst he was thankfully unhurt, the car was not repairable. It turned out the Hyundai had been spun around by a wayward Seat at Klostertal, the resulting contact with the barrier causing serious rear suspension damage which could not be fixed at the track. The Schumann team had to withdraw from the race, but I must admit feeling some sense of relief: over that week, I had picked up some really aggressive kind of flu bug which meant my joints were agonisingly painful. Getting in and out of the car was increasingly difficult and for this reason that phone call was something of a blessing.

For 2009, I wanted to move forward into faster classes at the Nürburgring and with the help of my Europcar-abusing friend Lars, I secured a seat in the Carlsson-backed Mercedes CK35 RS, in the hotly-contested SP6 class. As detailed earlier this was a tough race, the steering failure at Klostertal halfway through ultimately followed by a terminal engine failure through the fast curves after Pflanzgarten, with just five hours to go. Nevertheless, that year brought what is undoubtedly the most significant watershed moment in my racing career at a different 24 hour event altogether, a life-changing reward for all my faithful perseverance!

MEETING THE KING

In late May 2009, I was driving back from a business meeting in Banbury along the B4035, a rather fun cross-country route, when I pulled over into a rough layby a few miles north of Brailes to take a phone call from Matthias, then my boss at Dow Automotive. He proceeded to inform me that one of our company directors, who was due to fly to Le Mans the following week, had fallen down the stairs and "hurt his ass!" His doctor had advised him not to sit on a long-haul flight from Detroit, so would I please attend Le Mans in his place, along with our president? You can imagine I had already said yes before he'd even finished the question. My racing career had flat-lined somewhat and here was another opportunity to open up some doors!

The main Le Mans connection for Dow Automotive in that period was a diesel particulate-filter technology employed by the victorious Audi R10 since 2006 and subsequently the winning Peugeot 908 HDi FAP prototype class cars. The technology enabled effective filtration with minimal back-pressure and power loss. Head of Audi Motorsport, Dr Wolfgang Ullrich even wanted to hold a white-gloved hand behind the exhaust to show how clean the diesel emissions could be! We had meetings lined up with management from those teams to progress the technology development. Dow Automotive also had technology interests in the structural adhesives and composites space; for this reason, we also had arranged discussions with the Corvette and Aston Martin GT teams. This last meeting was the life-changer for me.

We sat down with Dr Ulrich Bez, then CEO of Aston Martin, in a hot and very noisy hospitality tent, just adjacent to Virage Ford. Dr Bez was an inspirational figure, charismatic and sharp. In spite of his long and impressive history with Porsche and BMW, I knew him mainly as a keen racing driver, having already competed against him at Nürburgring 24 hours races for several years. On the most recent occasion a month prior, amongst 170 starters, he and his team had impressively finished 21st overall in a V12 Vantage, Dr Bez aged 65!

After the usual introductions, our Dow president proceeded to the business talk, something that I could see held little interest for Ulrich as he looked about the tent. Against the backdrop of screaming race engines (or the deeper hissing rumble of those diesels), I stepped in with, "Congratulations on your success in the *real* 24 hours!" He fixed me with his icy stare and asked me what I meant. I explained we'd been on track together at the Green Hell not a month before and he immediately became animated, remembering the Carlsson Mercedes and for the next 15 minutes recounting the various challenges of the race. Watching us, our president looked like a spectator at Wimbledon, head turning back and forth as Ulrich and I exchanged great memories.

As our meeting time ended, I distinctly remember my words to Ulrich: "What do I have to do to drive with you at the Nürburgring?" This was my Jason Plato Frank Williams car park moment. He said,

"Give me your card." I really didn't think this would amount to much, having experienced so many knock-backs on the way to finding support for my racing ambitions. A few weeks later, I received a meeting invitation from someone who I will never be able to thank enough for the trust he later placed in me, Aston Martin Head of Special Projects, David King.

I didn't think anything was unusual about this meeting request: Dow Automotive had a lot of adhesive business with Aston Martin (their cars were structurally bonded together long before others in the industry followed suit) and it was not unusual to visit Gaydon to discuss new projects. I arrived, dutifully dressed in my suit and tie and began to talk about Dow's technology portfolio. Across the desk, David let me talk for about ten minutes and then he said with a smile, "You have no idea why you're here, have you?" I must confess, my heart was pounding as he explained he held a dual role at Aston Martin, including Head of Motorsport. On the recommendation of Dr Bez and after researching my racing history, he wanted me to do a test at the Nürburgring, to evaluate my capabilities in consideration for a seat with their factory team!

The test was set up in October. I'd be piloting Aston Martin's beautiful racing-green V8 Vantage N24 around the Nordschleife. Conditions were atrocious, with freezing rain, very changeable conditions and a line of oil preventing any meaningful lap times. Even though I managed to walk headfirst into the glass door in the Aston Martin hospitality, I didn't put a foot wrong out on track and as a result, Aston Martin Engineering Race Team (as it was known at the time) gave me a dream offer to join their works endurance racing programme from 2010!

After almost two decades of struggle, I'd found a team who believed in me. Not just any team, but Aston Martin, the iconic British brand I'd adored from my childhood days, since watching the insane Aston Martin V8 GT of David Ellis racing at Oulton Park. And to do this at the Green Hell! Christmas certainly came early that year. To celebrate, I treated myself to a new livery for my helmet: I'd carried variations of my original 'garden shed' yellow-and-blue helmet design far enough and I felt this turn of fortune deserved a new look. This was also my first lid with built-in radio and I must say, it's a far more effective system than the moulded ear plugs I'd used prior, which aren't particularly comfortable, reliable or hygienic.

The following season, my first race with Aston Martin was the DMV 4 hours Nürburgring, round two of the VLN (in German, Veranstaltergemeinschaft Langstreckenpokal Nürburgring), nowadays the more simply-named NLS (Nürburgring Langstrecken Serie). I would share the more powerful but heavier V12 Vantage with Wolfgang and Ulrich. We qualified fourth in the SP8 class, just behind the C6 Corvette which I was able to pass off the start, thanks to a good tyre warm-up strategy on the out lap. Our thundering V12 climbed the order to finish a tremendous second in class, behind the Gazoo Racing factory Lexus LFA driven by Armin Hahne, Kazuya Ohshima and Jochen Krumbach. As a boy, I was inspired by watching pro-driver Armin Hahne (with Jeff Allam) piloting the TWR Bastos Rover SD1 Vitesse around Silverstone in the 1985 Tourist Trophy; thanks to the excellent relationship between Aston Martin and Toyota/Lexus, we were now sharing one of the huge pit garages 25 years later! It was an honour to introduce myself to him.

The main event we'd been working towards was in May, the V12 Vantage now adorned with front splitter and rear wing to help transfer more of that power to the asphalt around the 80 plus corners of each lap in the 2010 Nürburgring 24 hours race. Sadness hung over the car's debut in April, with the aforementioned tragic death of our team mate, and the whole team had Leo in our thoughts as we arrived.

I would share the car with Chris Porritt, Oliver Mathai and Dickie Meaden, who wrote a great review of the car in EVO Magazine. To prove its amazing sportscar credentials, a four-door Rapide would also run, piloted by Dr Bez, Wolfgang Schubauer and Matthew Marsh, with Chris Porritt doubling up on driving duties. After a wet, foggy and unbelievably cold (4°C!) Thursday, with gloves and hats in evidence up and down the pit lane, Oli qualified us third in class in the dry session on Friday, thanks to a good slipstream and 'many oversteer moments'!

The race itself was straightforward, the car climbing inside the top 30 overall and into the class lead as the pole-sitting Lexus LFA encountered mechanical troubles. I made the mistake of being too enthusiastic about my first night stint, which resulted in David putting me back in for a double-stint through the graveyard shift until 3:30am. I came in only to find out Oli had been taken ill: I'd be required back behind the wheel again at 7:15am. I had no issue with that! It is always a treat to drive the Nordschleife in the early morning; the air is still cool, most of the maniacs have crashed out and we can get on with

197

the serious business of moving up the order. Our progress was briefly delayed with a driveshaft issue, the team replacing it in an incredible 16 minutes, and we emerged still in the class lead just ahead of the Lexus.

Unfortunately, the elation would only last a further lap. Exiting the Mini-Karussell, I powered up the hill as usual and the engine just died. I radioed in and we tried all the usual routines to reset the ECU but it just would not fire. In the end I had to be towed off the track just beyond Döttinger Höhe (on this track, it's very important to insist your tow-truck crew leaves you where you can be reached) and waited for the team to appear. David, together with two mechanics, jumped into the brand-new Aston Martin Cygnet display car and roared through the paddock to the VIP Parking area, where they transferred into Dr Bez's DBS, appearing at Döttinger Höhe within ten minutes of me being towed off track. I couldn't believe how fast they arrived! They got stuck into all the electronics but nothing seemed to solve the problem. Then lead mechanic Dean dived arm's length into the fuel tank to check the fuel pumps and found that was where the problem lay. Within minutes, the Vantage was being towed back to the paddock behind the DBS, (maybe the only time anyone has seen this spectacle!), the team replacing the fuel pump in the relative calm of the truck awning. Unbelievably, we went back out there, lapping at near qualifying pace and recovered to third in class by the flag! To add to our delight, the Rapide had enjoyed a steady and trouble-free run all the way to second in class, behind the all-conquering Lexus LFA of Armin, Jochen and Andre Lotterer.

The after-party in the Aston Martin corner of the famous Cockpit Bar of the Dorint Am Nürburgring was fantastic, with far too many appearances of the old 'Eifelgeist' spirit and accompanying white gloves! The president of Toyota, Akio Toyoda-san and his team were celebrating there with us and somewhere I still have a fabulous photograph of his enthusiastic karaoke performance, together with a very happy Ulrich Bez.

Getting home after the 24 hours proved to be a challenge as the Iceland Eyjafjallajökull volcano had gone pop, chucking ash into the sky and cancelling my Ryanair flight home. Fortunately, I discovered this just in time to grab a lift back to the UK with Aston Martin's Brand Communications Manager John Muirhead. I realised the long road trip was a great way to get to know the team better. Since that time, I've travelled by car to the 'Ring, almost always with David King, who over the years has become a great and trusted friend. For ten seasons we drove there and back together, putting together plans for future racing, our journey punctuated by the mildly-amusing Belgian place names like Aarschot, Catsop, or the classic Plopsaland. Maybe you had to be there!

David is an ex-rally navigator and very clock-conscious. When we left the 'Ring on a return journey, he already had a Channel Tunnel crossing time in mind and allowed 'pit stops' that only took as long as refuelling! On one early journey, before we really knew each other well enough, I managed to get a terrible stomach-ache holding in a fart for hours and hours, thanks to his rigorous travel schedule! I blame that Chunnel egg sandwich!

Typically, we'd use an ordinary SUV or MPV for those trips, but sometimes we'd take a prototype out there as an extended road test. Once we drove a prototype Vantage, a GT8 I think it was. It was very stripped out and noisy, with little in the way of interior trim, a lot of data boxes here and there to catch your trousers on and seats that frankly had no business in a car. In fact, we had to stuff clothes under our backsides to stop the numb-ness! After the trip, my eldest daughter clamoured for me to drive her to school in that car; unfortunately, it stuck in gear on our sloping drive and by the time we'd sorted out the problem, the school bell had rung and there was nobody around to see her when we finally arrived!

Back to 2010, in October we returned to a very wet Green Hell with two V12 Vantages for the DMV 250 Meilen Rennen, taking first and third place in the SP8 class. For Chris and I, it was a truly satisfying win, not only because it made up for our missed opportunity in May, but also because it was enabled by an inspired intermediate tyre choice on a drying track to catch and pass the leading Corvette of Sascha Bert and Duncan Huisman. I found Hatzenbach damp and then Flugplatz completely saturated all the way through Schwedenkreuz, Fuchsrohre and beyond, only drying around Kallenhard. The inters were working well once I got them up to temperature, but through the wet sections the heat was falling away and it was really slippery. It was a relief to find dry sections to recover tyre temperatures. In fact, it was a lot of fun to hassle and pass the normally quicker Audi R8s and Porsches who were struggling with their wet tyres in those drier sections.

As the rain intensified and cars began to aquaplane between Hatzenbach and Metzgesfeld, we made exactly the right call timing to switch to wets. Whether the Corvette drivers were attempting to respond to our attack, or whether they were simply caught out by the lack of grip, their race ended at Fuchsrohre, a notorious crash zone where a severe compression (taken in sixth gear) gathers rain water just where the track begins to curve. The first I knew about it was a slick of oil running up to the following chicane at Adenauer-Forst. I couldn't see which car it was thanks to all the rain and spray, but the team came on the radio a short while later and informed me it was the Corvette: we were leading the class! With the rain becoming torrential, the spray was becoming a major hazard, with zero visibility, just whiteness on the main straight. The organisers quickly elected to red-flag the race, handing us our class win with ten minutes remaining on the clock!

Such are the conditions the Green Hell has in store. Apart from anything else, it makes packing suitable clothes a difficult choice every time! I went on to enjoy nine further years of Nürburgring 24 hours races and other endurance events with Aston Martin, driving a wonderful variety of cars.

In 2012, together with Aussie Bathurst specialist Mal Rose, we took third place in the SP8 class in a V8 Vantage. This was quickly overshadowed when shockingly, team mate Jürgen Stumpf passed away soon after, during a hunting trip in Germany. Jürgen was a super guy, very genuine, experienced and passionate about his racing. We were exchanging emails on the Tuesday and a day later he was gone. It meant a lot that we were able to enjoy his final 24 hour race together and to bring home a top result.

2013 was more memorable for the Aston Martin centenary. Daniel Craig arrived in secrecy by helicopter just before the race and was ushered through the 'secret' press tunnel under the track to drive the James Bond 'Skyfall' DB5 along with 99 other cars on a celebration parade lap. For me however, the greater thrill was sitting across from Sir Stirling Moss and his wife Lady Susie at breakfast in the hotel. He was there to pilot the DBR1 in which he triumphed at the 1958 and 1959 Nürburgring 1000km.

The Nürburgring 24 hours race on this occasion started amidst sunshine but ominous black clouds circled the track in all directions, spitting vengeance for the earlier clear qualifying conditions. Our V12 Vantage was running well, but mid-evening, as I changed down just before Schwalbenschwantz, the car suddenly died. No engine, no gears, nothing! I tried all the usual reset procedures but it was clear something major had upset the electronics and there was no choice but to wait to be recovered. The race was red-flagged shortly before 11pm due to atrocious weather. Despite a restart at 8:20am, we had lost so much time identifying the electronics problem (eventually traced to a tiny failed ECU contact), all chance of a decent result was lost. At least Mal was able to grab another third-place finish in our sister V8 Vantage, after his team mate (crazy cigar-smoking truck-racer Egon 'egon off again' Allgäuer), suffered damage from a heavy crash that was able to be repaired during the red-flag period.

In 2014, we went one better with a second-place SP8 finish in the Exide-backed V12 Vantage (with Marcus Mahy, Liam Talbot and Egon), despite losing five laps to repairs after the lead McLaren struck the rear of our car. However, the real high-points of this time with Aston Martin were the victories we enjoyed together: the SP8 class win in 2017 driving the Vantage GT8 (with Darren Turner, Nicky Thiim and Markus Lungstrass) and then the SP8T class win in 2019 in the debut year of the new Vantage (with Alex Brundle and Jamie Chadwick).

Over this same period, David also asked me to drive the GT8 at a few one-off events which were truly memorable. First, in November 2017, we flew over to COTA near Austin in Texas, to contest the SP3 class in the 24H Series. My team mates were Aston Martin CEO Andy Palmer (Dr Bez having stepped down in 2013), the incomparable and very genuine John Hindhaugh (the dulcet Mackem tones of Radio Le Mans) who I'd known for a while, and celebrity TV baker (and keen racer) Paul Hollywood, who I didn't know at all.

We met up in the lounge at Heathrow and Paul was immediately very approachable and open with me; I was a bit surprised at this until he apologised and said it was because I looked just like his best mate! Nevertheless, he was a lot of fun to be around, especially considering the stress the red tops were putting him under that weekend. As Ricky Bobby would say, it was 'shake and bake' for us in COTA, leading the class until Paul suffered a suspension failure over one of the aggressive apex kerbs at Turn 8. Nevertheless, we recovered to finish second in class behind the Porsche Cayman of Freddie Hunt and Co. The event was unusual in that it was split into two sections, the cars in *parc-fermé* overnight, allowing us all to enjoy the wonderful Austin hospitality together on Saturday evening!

In 2018, Andy and I shared the GT8 at the Circuit De La Sarthe on the weekend of Le Mans 24 hours. A highlight was passing Martin Brundle's GT4 around the outside into Virage Porsche, something I would never attempt with a less experienced opponent! The race was sadly blighted by a seemingly endless safety-car period, thanks to a stupidly aggressive GT3 driver ploughing into another GT4 which ended up in the wall further into the Porsche Curves. Later that season in October, we also took the GT8 to Spa for the 24H Series 12-hour race there, Andy and I sharing with the very competitive Sir Chris Hoy (and a rather alarming intermittently malfunctioning headlight). Apart from his impressive speed behind the wheel, I have two other enduring memories of Chris, the first being the size of his thighs: one of them was the size of my waist! I honestly don't know how he could squeeze them into that race seat. The second was his use of that strength when our camp fire was in danger of expiring at Le Mans: Chris appeared from a nearby field carrying an entire haybale single-handed that certainly reignited the evening!

A decade with Aston Martin and later Aston Martin Racing was a golden era for me. I was integrated into a supportive team which elevated my driving to a new level, thanks to working with some of the world's best pro-drivers, engineers and mechanics. All good things come to an end of course. By early 2020, Andy Palmer had long departed, billionaire Lawrence Stroll took a major stake in Aston Martin and the company refocussed its endurance racing efforts through partner teams. COVID-19 then raised its ugly head: just getting to the Nürburgring that year was a victory in itself, as it was in 2021 (especially with UK Border Force only accepting COVID-19 test results in English, French and Spanish but not German!).

Aston Martin understandably elected not to risk their team's health by travelling to Germany at that time. However, I wanted to continue my unbroken run of Nürburgring 24 hours race starts, so I jumped brands to Porsche, achieving a brace of SP4T class wins (with Köppen Motorsport) and a second-place Cup 3 class finish (with Mathol Racing), but the spell had been broken. David King left for Fisker in 2021 and the last remnants of those glorious Aston Martin years faded into the forests of the Green Hell.

SHOW ME THE MONEY

My return to privateer status in 2020 was a stark reminder of the budgetary realities faced by racing drivers. Even if my track record brought advantageous offers, I was now in my fifties and finding support to cover my costs was far more difficult than in my younger years.

Funding is the real fuel of motorsport. Even at the very top of the sport, many drivers are obliged to bring substantial monies to access or maintain their race seats. Of course, they will be at great pains to avoid the career-limiting label of 'pay driver' with some smoke-and-mirrors whereby their personal sponsor is portrayed as a team sponsor. When their money dries up however, any talent they have shown to that point will have to compete with the queue of replacement drivers and sponsors waiting in the paddock hospitality.

Races may be won by the best drivers, but championships are won by the best funded. This was already obvious to me at privateer club racing level. If we were shunted off the track by another wealthier driver, he'd be back racing at the next event, whilst we would be out for a few races until we could afford to repair the car. This financial constraint changes the driver's attitude on track and as we've already discussed, the cost of a cautious approach is measured in vital tenths and lost podiums.

Teams operate on a larger scale but like privateers, they are also budget-limited. They are businesses with financial commitments like any other and will usually prioritise their short-term need for positive cashflow above their longer-term desire to achieve all-conquering success. This is the unspoken reality of motor racing, particularly in lower categories. It's getting ever rarer to find a team who values talent above money, even if teams at the Nürburgring's Green Hell have been an exception due to the extreme risks of hiring an incompetent driver there. Business priorities are also one of the reasons why Pro-Am racing has grown into a successful model: a wealthy Am brings the necessary funds, a talented Pro brings the lap time and the wins. Unfortunately, those Ams' wallets have also pushed up the price of a race seat to ridiculous levels, especially at prestigious events like Le Mans. They can often lap pretty competitively too, because as we know, a well-engineered car plays a large part in the overall success of the package!

There is a famous adage that is relevant here: "How do you make a small fortune in motorsport? Start with a large one." I realised already at Team Touraco in the late 1980s that I would not be able to self-fund an entry into even the lowest echelons of modern one-make racing. The first trick then was to find someone else to pay as soon as possible. I must have written hundreds, if not thousands of letters to prospective sponsors through the 1990s, most of the time receiving no acknowledgement whatsoever (one of the more notable and kind exceptions being from a certain Mr Eddie Jordan).

I worked with marketing professionals to help me pitch the details of the available sponsorship packages behind the proposals. There is an expectation that a professional driver will have representation; it's an illusion which gives the impression of a wider belief in the driver's talents and career aspirations. However, this was a frustrating experience for me because I found I could better represent the sponsor benefits myself, having lived and breathed the paddock for so many seasons. When we lost Anadin Ultra over the winter of 2000, I would say a significant portion of the responsibility lay with the poor showing from the 'professional' who accompanied me to the presentation, despite all our preparations beforehand.

I used my old design skills to illustrate the race car with the potential sponsor's logos, detailing the various costs of the decal locations and sizes. As things became more serious, I even enlisted the considerable graphics talents of Coventry alumnus Andy Blackmore, race car livery designer and producer of the artwork behind Spotters Guides. Even if they didn't trigger the necessary deals to prolong my BTCC dream, I still have some of his superb creative artwork from this period, including a memorable image on the race car door of a lingerie-clad figure in the ideal driving position. The target was a certain adult entertainment club, a sponsor that today would undoubtedly cause offence, but the example demonstrates the desperation of a driver chasing a budget.

After my years in Fiestas unsuccessfully hunting for a deal of sufficient magnitude to propel me to the next level, I came to realise I needed to better leverage what made me unique and appealing to potential sponsors. My best option was right in front of me: my employer, Dow Automotive! I owe a great deal of thanks to Dennis McGrew, our Commercial Director in Frankfurt at the time, who listened carefully to my proposition for company involvement and how I was best placed to represent our business interests. He judged it on merit, rather than as a perk for an employee. His willingness to invest opened the door to my drives with Barwell Motorsport and made it appreciably easier to convince other companies such as Dexter Corporation, Magna International and even others outside the automotive field who could see the pedigree of my sponsors. It's worth noting their interest was sometimes motivated by the opportunity to forge business relationships with our existing sponsors.

In those early days of my corporate life at Dow, I learned how to quantify the marketing exposure benefits in terms of international reach, broadcast hours, viewing audience figures, their socio-economic profile and suchlike. As I progressed to higher categories of racing, these factors became much greater influences. It was a lot easier to sell a BTCC package with 40,000 spectators or a Nürburgring package with 250,000 spectators, than it was to interest a company in club racing events attended by a few thousand die-hard fans in muddy wellies. From my perspective, the required sponsorship at this level seemed unachievable initially, but to a blue-chip corporation, the numbers were almost inconsequential within their overall marketing budget.

The most immediate and obvious attraction for these sponsors was the opportunity to gain massive TV and (in those days) print media coverage, with high-profile public advertising of their products or service brands through the placement of decals on the race cars, driver overalls, team clothing and the team race transporter, all of which travelled the length and breadth of the country through the racing season. With the emergence of the digital world, added exposure on the team website and even on the official championship website was also of value. In addition to providing an ideal platform for a successful marketing and communications campaign, we'd include the now commonplace offer to create promotional items bearing the image of the sponsor's logo or brands, such as team posters, clothing, videos or even product samples, which could be distributed at the race events or other venues.

At Barwell Motorsport, we enjoyed support from Red Devil energy drink, developed in the Netherlands in the mid-1990s as a competitor to Red Bull. Cases of sample cans were brought to the events and we'd always have a can in our hands at photoshoots or race events. I even recall a promotional campaign where a stunt rider jumped a BMX over our heads as we nonchalantly sipped our Red Devils. I must confess I couldn't actually drink the stuff: I'd empty out the contents and fill the can full of water at the first opportunity!

Barwell were incorrigible pranksters: when team mate Jason Yeomans' main sponsor Turtle Wax were invited to the paddock tent for a show around his Vectra, the team had meticulously added a 'Monkey Boy' decal to the car, on the sill so Jason would see it only when he opened the door. I never did learn why that was his nickname, but watching him try to keep a straight face in front of his guests was priceless!

Hospitality opportunities were (and still are) a crucial part of effective sponsorship packages, especially for business-to-business companies, where TV or public exposure is not necessarily a major draw. Then as now, there were first-class facilities to cater for our sponsors and their guests, with exclusive trackside viewing area, sit-down lunch, waiter service, complementary bar and live entertainment, including driver interviews. There were package deals to be done with the hospitality companies, leaving more of my precious sponsorship funds available for running the race car. Quantifying the benefits for business-to-business companies is more difficult than for consumer products, but I did enjoy one outcome at Oulton Park, after the customer guests of my sponsor Dexter Corporation enjoyed the available alcohol rather too much and wrecked a part of the hospitality tent. Their manager was apparently so embarrassed, he awarded several hundred thousand pounds-worth of business to Dexter, which more than covered their season's investment!

For such sponsors, I'd also make myself available for off-track events and talks, for example at industry exhibitions or team-building events. Once again in support of Dexter, I remember persuading Chris at Barwell to join me in Manchester for an exhibition I think was named RubberEx or similar. On arriving at GMEX, he was supremely disappointed to find out it was focused on industrial rubber moulding, not on personal apparel!

Whenever I found a company decision-maker with a passion for racing, I'd include more personal options in the proposal, such as a race-day tour with yours truly. There was enormous value in bringing guests into the inner sanctum of the pit garage and showing them the workings of the team and the race car. Imagine their response when, back in the real world of their office the following Monday, they'd find in their inbox their photograph (or even better, one of their son or daughter), sitting in the race car the previous day. Where possible, I was always happy to have enthusiastic guests accompany me on my track walk during the evening prior to race day. They would always appreciate hair-raising descriptions of impossible overtaking moves, the experience being so much more tangible astride the skid marks at different points around the circuit.

Returning to the crucial involvement of Dow with my racing activities, this was initially relatively short-lived. After my curtailed BTCC campaigns with Barwell Motorsport and Team B&Q Jet York City, Dow entered a period of serious financial crisis and there was no prospect of further support. This was one of the primary reasons for my refocus on GT racing, with the budget being shared between multiple drivers, the split ideally depending on talent! It was only in 2016, when I had been racing with Aston Martin for several seasons, that Dow came back on board once again, albeit under quite a different business model than previously.

Inspired by a 'technical partnership' Dow had established with Richard Childress Racing (RCR) in NASCAR, I could see a similar opportunity was viable with Aston Martin, who had already partnered with Castrol to develop a new oil-change system under the Nexcel brand. We spent a lot of time working with the Nexcel engineers, testing the system on track ahead of commercial launch. The premise is the same even in Formula 1: technology brought by sponsor partners is developed and tested in the rigorous racing environment.

Aston Martin were already a customer of Dow Automotive and it was in the interest of both parties to explore new technology areas which addressed the most pressing industry needs in the area of fuel efficiency, light-weighting and the like. Aston Martin were significantly more agile than the larger car makers and could involve partners to validate the technology much more rapidly than would otherwise be possible for Dow alone. With the guidance of David King, we formalised a technical partnership which continued even after I left Dow early in 2018, their investment also funding Aston Martin's World Endurance Championship (WEC) campaign. Frustratingly, the stars did not align for me in this respect: it would have been a dream for me to compete in the Vantage GTE but, as David poignantly said to me after we won the Nürburgring SP8T class together in 2019, "It's a shame this didn't happen for you earlier." In other words, age was now my career constraint.

Even if disproving that ageist theory has been a major motivation for me since, such missed opportunities are still painful to recall, even if they were not evident at the time. Back in my Vectra days at Brands Hatch, I approached Mike Nicholson (then Vauxhall Motorsport Operation Manager) about obtaining some additional tyres. When I stood up to leave, he said, "I thought you were going to ask me for something else!" Like a fool, I didn't pick up on the remote possibility that a test in one of his works BTCC Astras might have been on the cards; my career could have taken an entirely different direction, with or without Dow backing. Sometimes we drive too fast along our road and miss a vital junction...

As mentioned previously, Dow's interest in WEC was based on their development of diesel particulate filter technology. At Le Mans, I think in 2007, they had invited over from America three Cummins vice-presidents, great guys and really enthusiastic petrol-heads (or maybe diesel-heads?). During the race, as midnight approached in the hospitality unit, the Dow folks were looking towards their beds but the Cummins team were having none of that! They were going to do the full 24 hours and it wasn't a great strain for me to volunteer as their guide. We walked over towards the Mulsanne Straight, dodging officious French security guards and slipping through the dark woods guided only by the light of an old Nokia mobile phone until we were right behind the Armco. I must say that semi-illegal trackside experience counts as one of my most memorable outside a race car. Things were topped off perfectly when, as tiredness hit us at about 3am, one of my guests said, "Don't worry, I grabbed some energy drinks from the hospitality!" Fumbling in the dark, it was only when I glugged several mouthfuls that I realised in fact he'd picked up cans of Stella Artois!

Although there is a lot of value (and fun) to be had trackside, there is nothing better in my opinion than getting your sponsors and their guests out on to the race track itself, where they can drive and be driven, learning first-hand the secrets of high-speed lapping and car control. These events were also valuable in progressing the sponsor relationship to the next level. Sponsorship decision-makers are busy people, but as I used to say, "A track day is theirs but their time is yours!" Usually, track days were conducted in road cars, with all the expected grip and performance limitations. An exception was the VLN events at the Nürburgring where the actual race car could be fitted with a temporary passenger seat, allowing guests to experience a white-knuckle lap at pretty much racing speed, amongst lots of other race cars, on a Friday afternoon before the race weekend.

It wasn't always plain sailing though: on one occasion, a young lady climbed aboard the Aston Martin's passenger seat and after a short introduction whilst she was strapped in, we accelerated out of the pit lane. I always use a thumbs-up thumbs-down system if we have no radio, to make sure the guest is happy. In this case, even before we'd approached the first corner, she was frantically giving me the thumbs down! I thought her belts must have opened or something, so I pulled off the line to the right around the hairpin and looked across to see her face, white and shaking with fear! It was simply not for her. Ironically, we then had to drive super-slowly around the lap with cars whipping by, a far more dangerous scenario than a lap at normal speeds.

That same day, I had a German guest join me and he was double-thumbs-up the whole time. In the evening Aston Martin had arranged to meet our guests for dinner in the hotel, but this gentleman didn't show up. We called his room and he said he'd see us at breakfast. I only found out then that he had felt very unwell after his passenger lap, having had open heart surgery only a few months before! I still shudder to think of the possible consequences...

The most fearless passengers I can recall participated at a Mission Motorsport track day at Goodwood where I was attending for Aston Martin. It's clear that at any track day, we typically don't drive at 100%, even if it feels like it from the passenger seat. At Goodwood however, those military veterans were not impressed unless I hung it out on the ragged edge! I assume their frame of reference was far more traumatic than anything I could conjure behind the wheel.

To some extent, karting events are another way to allow us to share the racing experience with sponsors. Most of the time we'd arrange a mix of teams so we were not racing directly against the guys paying the bills! On one occasion however, we had a French customer who expressed to my colleague Stephane and I his desire to go karting. Stephane was quite a competitive character but neither of us felt it would be correct to pass our customer! We roughed each other up just behind him, getting more and more aggressive in our battle to occupy second place without driving too fast. When our guest took the chequered flag and then saw the state of our karts, I guess he thought he'd driven the race of the century!

I still truly enjoy driving on track days, but I must say, being driven by a guest has never brought me any pleasure at all. When my mates asked me to arrange a trip over the Green Hell to have a bit of rent-a-race-car fun, I was glad to oblige but for the laps where they wanted to drive, I contacted my old Norwegian friend Lars to instruct them, whilst I enjoyed a Bitburger on the balcony of the Devil's Diner! I'd previously spent time as a Porsche Driver Consultant when Porsche opened their centre at Silverstone, but gave it up after too many near

217

misses with guest drivers whose ambition exceeded their talent. Of course, in theory it was up to us as instructors to control their speed but some folks just would not listen. If I felt they were putting me at risk, I'd simply ask them to pull over and then spend an overly long time filling in their assessment paperwork!

As I realised from my various corporate positions, it certainly helps a driver's sponsorship prospects to be able to converse about more than just motorsport. There are in fact many parallels between endurance racing and the business world. There are various accounts of how companies and service industries have observed professional race teams to learn how to optimise their operations. To fall into business-speak for a moment, racing and business share similar ideals such as the need for effective team work, alignment around common goals, detailed understanding of complex issues, respect and integrity in the face of intense competition and most importantly how to enjoy winning together. If this sounds a little dull, suck it up! Don't step into the arena unless you have the weapons to win the battle. As the representative of my sponsors' brands, I researched their business goals, their products and learned to speak their corporate language. It made my partnership proposals immeasurably more powerful, compelling and marketable.

Take for example the support of Tregothnan, British tea grower and tea merchant, which I enjoyed for several years, mainly because I understood their vision. The partnership was actually triggered by a chance exchange on Twitter. They were initially attracted by the British heritage and prestige associated with Aston Martin, but after our discussions, I could see a link between tea's advantageous slow caffeine release and endurance racing's requirement for sustained alertness. A collaboration made sense for everyone involved. Tregothnan products were made available to Aston Martin hospitality guests, elevating brand awareness and status. The Radio Le Mans team at the time was hosted by Aston Martin; John Hindhaugh and Eve Hewitt would always kindly advocate the 'restorative powers of Tregothnan', a few complementary boxes of their Great British tea helping the commentary team's alertness through the 24 hour events. A substantial add-on perk for me were relaxing breaks in Tregothnan's beautiful and very peaceful holiday houses at Coombe in Cornwall, across the River Fal from the Tregothnan estate. If you have the good fortune to visit, their tea grows on the hillsides above.

Sometimes desperation to maintain funding of a racing career may lead a driver down some crazy avenues. Even after I'd been kicked out of John Batchelor's BTCC team, he called me up to his 'castle' residence in the northwest of England and through the fog of countless cigarettes, he informed me of a plan to race NASCAR. He'd worked out that simply turning up to qualify could potentially earn hundreds of thousands of dollars of start money, even if we pulled off the track after the start. I declined John's offer of course, but such madcap, highly-questionable and even illegal schemes have been seriously entertained or put into practice when budget is lacking, such as the widely-reported cocaine-smuggling operation of one BTCC team, allegedly enabled by frequent use of Zandvoort as a testing venue in the 1990s.

Racing itself is horribly addictive, success tantalisingly close and costs somehow justifiable until the podiums dry up. I can entirely sympathise with the desolation of drivers who fall off the funding ladder before they can show their talent in a top-level category. Given that such career opportunities usually come when a driver is of a relatively young age, being out of a drive at that stage is like watching your only candle burn down in broad daylight. It's a frustrating wasteful experience. My own opportunity with Aston Martin came much later in my career than I wished, but I hope my story shows that professionalism and determination, even a degree of stubbornness, can eventually bring rewards without resorting to illicit practices, however impossible it may seem.

HARD DRIVING

I believe I may have lived through a golden era of motorsport. Maybe others have said this before me, preferring the time before aerodynamic domination. Maybe others will say it far into the future, when race cars are no longer driven by humans. Our personal views are mainly fuelled by nostalgia of course, and it's sometimes difficult to let go of the elements we consider fundamental to those 'better times'.

With social and political attention firmly fixed upon climate change in most regions, it's no surprise that motorsport has come under scrutiny. I will focus heavily here on Formula 1, because it exerts a strong influence over motorsport regulatory direction in general, and over recent decades has positioned itself as the pinnacle of automotive technology in order to attract the major car makers. That technology needs to be relevant to the wider automotive market, with its interest in exhaust emissions and fuel efficiency. Consequently, fuel capacity restrictions have been implemented to force development of more efficient internal combustion engines. In reality, these measures have prevented flat-out driving, a significant negative for the quality of the racing. Who could ever have imagined 'lift-and-coast' would be an essential skill of a racing driver?

Similarly, technical regulations have led to the emergence of all manner of hybrid- or full-electric powertrains which not only deliver their power differently, but also sound less impressive to the traditional trackside spectator. That may not matter to the younger generations who never heard the scream of the Formula 1 Ferrari V8, V10 or V12 (before the hybrid regulations were introduced in 2014) or the iconic Mazda 787b Group C sportscar with its spine-tingling rotary engine. There was an audible relationship between power and speed. My personal favourite was the rumble-in-the-chest of the Corvette C6 R which just oozed torque, turning heads every lap it passed us at Le Mans in 2006. Somehow, I struggle to pick up the same vibes from the bespoke full-electric powertrains of Formula E, a sound I heard disparagingly described as "like a washing machine on full spin." That's not to denigrate the racing spectacle Formula E can offer: the category does tick several important boxes as I'll explain.

An underlying issue for motor racing in general is the premise that the highest echelons of the sport must be the fastest. Why should that be? The answer is rooted in early automotive history, when speed records caught the headlines. As a school-boy with a pack of Top Trumps in my pocket, road and race cars alike were judged on their top speed. Even today we expect to see lap records broken, as if that is a sign of progress. The problem this has created is an inflexibility in the structure of the sport. It becomes difficult to implement regulations to significantly slow Formula 1 cars for example, because the Formula 2 cars could then be faster at the same event. Formula 2 chassis and engine regulations are fixed for multiple years for cost reasons, as are those for Formula 3 and so there is an unhelpful interrelationship inhibiting change.

Much as I love driving at pace the unrestricted sections of German autobahns (rare as they are becoming), top speed is essentially irrelevant on the majority of public roads today, mainly due to overcrowded traffic conditions and the proliferation of speed limits (even if modern cars are considerably safer than their older generation counterparts). If motorsport is to truly reflect automotive market needs, perhaps we can slightly curtail our obsession with speed in the interests of better racing? Stay with me here: I'm very aware I'm poking the bear!

The point of any sport is that it should be an unequivocal measure of who is the best competitor. Top golf tournaments for example are played on some of the most difficult courses, to establish who is the most skilful player; the informed crowd can appreciate the extreme talent they are witnessing. This is less and less the case with Formula 1. Even if the cars (and their steering wheels) have become more complex, it's not about how many buttons and dials the driver uses to extract the maximum from the car, it's about the obvious driving difficulty which should be clearly visible to onlookers trackside. Martin Brundle commented at Silverstone in 2023 that modern Formula 1 cars are much more 'trustworthy' (in other words, easier to drive) than those of his era and that's a shame for our sport. Each category on the motor racing ladder should become progressively more challenging to drive, but this does *not* mean they must necessarily be faster. Of course, increased speeds involve faster driver reactions, less margin for error, higher g-forces, supreme levels of athletic fitness and so on, but to a great degree the spectators' perception of these intricacies is lost as the difference between good and great becomes infinitesimal. Interestingly, Max Verstappen's ideas for future Formula 1 cars (also shared at Silverstone in 2023) included reversion to pure V8 combustion engines (presumably powered by synthetic 'green' fuel), even if they are slightly *slower* than the hybrid powertrain package.

Fortunately, there are some other basic attributes beyond speed, which elevate the driving challenge. First and most obvious is the relationship between power and grip. In my opinion, elite racing drivers should be confronted with excessive power for the available grip. Max too was advocating smaller tyres. We all know a low-grip wet track surface offers the most proficient drivers a winning opportunity, not to mention more entertaining racing for spectators, and nobody cares that the speeds are decreased in those conditions! Why should we have to pray for rain to ease the monotony of another Formula 1 race weekend? The grip level should be reduced by redefining the dry tyre compound and construction specifications, something that could be implemented across multiple categories to maintain the hierarchy of championship categories. Just look at the fabulous spectacle of the Australian Supercars Championship, their relatively narrow 280-width slicks having to transfer 620bhp to the tarmac from their throaty 5 litre V8s.

Lower-grip tyre regulations are also one of the positive aspects of Formula E. As you'll have read in the 7am Race-Craft chapter, even the most basic forms of racing benefit from this approach, such as our Fun

Cup endurance series adventures with hard-compound tyres which led to all manner of ludicrous slides. Thanks to low degradation, one set could complete half a 25-hour race before needing replacement. In the spirit of motor racing supporting relevant road car technology development, surely this is a more economical and environmentally friendly approach, rather than throwing on new tyres at every pit stop? An undesirable side effect of fewer tyre changes could then be cautious tyre management strategies with cars circulating far from the limit. To alleviate this, tyres need to be engineered to operate at a defined grip limit for the required race duration, as they are able to do in endurance racing; if the intended grip limit is lowered as I'm recommending, the tyre engineering challenge to achieve this durability is also reduced.

At this point, someone in the room will stand up and say, "Wait, if we reduce mechanical grip with harder tyres, aerodynamic downforce will dominate and cars won't be able to follow each other closely." True, so reduce the level of aero also! This is where I am at odds with Max. I'm not advocating zero aero but Formula E cars generate only about one-third of the downforce of a Formula 1 car, enabling super-close dices which frankly for me are the main attraction of their races. The complexity of Formula 1 aerodynamics and the level of downforce produced are mostly irrelevant to all but the most insane supercars on normal roads. Big aero creates big spray in wet conditions, leading to terrible visibility and subsequent accidents (recently the reason for investigations into use of 'wheel arches' for wet races). Furthermore, such aero packages are far too sensitive to damage on track. Granted, avoiding contact is a measure of driver skill, but the risk of a broken winglet ruining a race (for driver and spectator alike) is too great. There is an optimum to be reached of course; for example, I believe the great Indycar racing we've seen since 2018 is at least partially due to their lowered downforce levels. It's interesting to observe that multiple Australian Supercars champion Scott McLaughlin soon became a multiple winner in Indycar. Both categories now require a more visually exciting scruff-of-the-neck driving style; sadly, too much of this has been eradicated in modern Grand Prix cars.

Formula 1 has long known it has an over-reliance on aerodynamic grip. Since 2011 (and later in lower categories), a Drag Reduction System (called DRS or as I insist, a Difficulty Reduction System) was introduced to give an artificial aerodynamic advantage to following cars. Predictably, it didn't allow cars to follow any closer through corners and so the overtakes only came on the straights. Frankly, nobody should pay to see that: just stand on a motorway bridge and watch it for free. At the 2023 Singapore Grand Prix, DRS actually precluded what should have been a thrilling conclusion to the race. The leading Ferrari of Carlos Sainz backed off slightly to allow Lando Norris' McLaren to remain within the one second gap required to permit DRS. Smart as that may have been of Carlos, the resulting 'DRS train' denied the following two Mercedes a realistic chance to attack Lando for second place.

Even when it does enable a pass, DRS not only reduces overtaking skill levels, but prior to the contrived 'drive-by' pass, the drag reduction also gives the following car the further advantage of leveraging the ERS to recover more energy without losing time to the car ahead. This energy is then strategically deployed via the hybrid electric powertrain, the resulting power boost usually preventing the overtaking car from being re-passed, further depriving the fans. Of most concern however, DRS has allowed engineers to actually *increase* downforce from wing settings (making it even harder for other cars to follow through corners), knowing they would enjoy a bonus speed-increase in the DRS zones. New Formula 1 regulations in 2022 tried to address this by reducing the loss of aero grip in the wake behind other cars through generation of ground-effect downforce under the car. Surprisingly, DRS was still maintained: I suspect rule-makers were not confident enough in their regulation changes and concerned they might see no overtaking at all.

It appears that future Formula 1 regulations will include even more 'active' aerodynamic features, even employing non-driver-controlled moveable wings or retractable elements. This in my view is where we start to encounter a critical conflict with the intent of motorsport. Any non-competitor-controlled mechanism detracts from the purity of what we consider a sport, risks manipulation (that nobody likes) and confuses even the most well-informed enthusiasts.

There are powerful business interests exploiting Formula 1 and demanding that the 'show' be enhanced to grow the casual fan base. Nevertheless, sporting credibility must be preserved at its heart: the consequences of heart failure are clear to everyone. Whether aero- or powertrain-related, non-driver-controlled technological features that can overshadow driver performance, especially when they malfunction, cast doubt even upon the relevance of a driver's championship. The end-game of external control in motorsport would be autonomous race cars, *sans pilote*, something that holds no interest for me. I strongly believe, once the cars have left the pit lane, the drivers' actions must dominate the on-track duel, their decisions prompting success or failure. Regarding active aero, if it must be used, the range of high- and low-downforce settings should be fixed by driver and team ahead of each race. DRS zones should be eliminated, allowing the drivers to decide where they deploy low- or high-downforce around the lap. With these options available, we'd see some diverse strategies with some high-quality racing, and no longer have to suffer interminable TV replays of unimpressive DRS passes which are an insult to the intelligence of serious motor racing fans everywhere.

The evolution of active aero in principle is relevant to road cars in the interests of reducing drag, thereby minimising required engine power and consequent fuel consumption at elevated speeds. Consistent with my point about Indycar however, the highest downforce setting available should be significantly reduced, compared to what we see in Formula 1 today. This way, aero drag is also reduced (currently around three times higher than a typical road car), top speeds are increased and braking distances lengthened to expand overtaking opportunities. It's worth remembering however that downforce and drag have a squared relationship with speed: it doesn't require much of a speed increase to generate a whole lot more downforce. Equally, if the speed falls, the car will rapidly lose aero grip, eventually depending only on the mechanical grip available from the tyres. Racing categories that suffer from a 'valley of death' where mechanical grip is exceeded before aero grip builds sufficiently, are forced to respond with increased aero. This magnifies the disadvantage a following driver feels, the turbulent 'wake' behind the lead car often preventing positioning for an overtake and resulting in frustrating processional races, not only in Formula 1 but also in prototype sports cars and other high-downforce classes.

Overtaking is a fundamental component of an entertaining race. Most important for the spectacle and for driver satisfaction, the overtake should comprise at least one car going visibly close to (or even over) the limit of tyre adhesion. That means overtaking must happen on the brakes and/or in a corner. Short of employing reverse grids with points for qualifying, overtaking opportunities have to be instigated by design of the cars.

If tyre mechanical grip and aero have been optimised in this respect, car weight is the next aspect to consider. A heavier car takes longer to decelerate and is more challenging to control in the corners. These factors extend braking distances and offer more opportunities for the following driver to execute a pass. Why then are future Formula 1 regulations still focussing on reducing weight? Likely because, ever since the days of Colin Chapman, everyone in motorsport recognises that a lighter car is quicker, not to mention a whole lot of fun to drive!

When questioned about potential upcoming technical regulation changes during the 2023 Formula 1 summer break, FIA President Mohammed Ben Sulayem was widely reported to have said that lighter cars are better, from his experience driving rallies. Regardless, rally cars do not typically have to overtake one another! During the same interview, Mr Ben Sulayem was quoted as saying in an accident, more weight is more dangerous. Having worked for many years in the area of automotive crash safety, I can say the opposite is true: all else being equal, a lighter car will decelerate more rapidly than a heavier one when it strikes a barrier or other static object. This more abrupt transfer of impact forces to the driver increases the severity of the crash pulse and is more likely to result in driver soft-tissue damage or other injuries.

2023 Formula 1 cars are a little over 30% (200kg) heavier than their year 2000 counterparts, due to enhanced on-board impact safety features and the heavier hybrid power units. The argument to reduce the weight of Formula 1 cars somewhat matches automotive industry light-weighting goals for energy efficiency, yet modern full-electric road cars also weigh a little over 30% more than the equivalent internal combustion engine model (that's around a 500kg difference for a mid-size car), mainly due to their battery pack (also a significant part of the reason why Formula E cars are currently over 100kg heavier than Formula 1 cars). This average road car weight doesn't even include the approximate 10% increase in the last 20 years associated with engineering safety countermeasures to meet more stringent crash tests. Relatively speaking then, there should be no great societal pressure to reduce weight in Formula 1 or any other racing category. Even if Max or other drivers would prefer to drive a lighter car, the emphasis of the technical regulations should be on the racing, not driving pleasure.

The size of the cars is a final ingredient which can help or hinder overtaking. Clearly the narrower the vehicle, the greater the available space on a given circuit for side-by-side action. Witness any Moto GP race. What is perhaps less obvious is the influence of car length. The 7am Race-Craft chapter clarifies that the overtaking driver must have a significant portion of their car alongside their intended prey: it's harder to achieve this with a longer car. Formula 1 cars generate braking forces of up to 5g, as an example decelerating from 200mph (320kmh) to a little over 80mph (130kmh) over a distance of around 120 metres. That's approximately only 22 Formula 1 car lengths, in approximately 2 seconds! The difference between a driver getting 'significantly alongside' or ramming a front wheel into their adversary's rear is then marginal and any car length reduction will ease that challenge.

I'm sure experts in the field will accuse me of over-simplifying the case, but to summarise, relative to Formula 1, an ideal racing category for drivers and fans alike would feature reduced mechanical grip, less aerodynamic downforce and a shorter car length, with increased weight. I've just described every GT race car I have had the pleasure to drive, all of which I would argue offer a far higher quality of racing than Formula 1 in 2023 (and are far more relevant to road car development).

GT cars are by no means perfect racing cars but that's the point. They are compromises to varying degrees, depending upon the original donor car and this is what makes them such an enjoyable experience to watch trackside and to race. These imperfections require more involvement from the driver to compensate, and as a result there is more fulfilment to be gained, especially where there are fewer electronic driver aids (as mentioned in the 4am The Feeling chapter).

The kerb weight of these machines can be in the region of 1350kg to 1650kg, requiring a different driving style to manage the momentum, rotation and tyre wear in comparison to a single seater of less than half the weight. A more favourable mechanical grip ratio with aerodynamic downforce favours close following, and overtaking is aided by the longer braking distances. They generally sound incredible too! It's no wonder that most Pro drivers falling off the single seater ladder absolutely adore driving GT3, GTE and the like, even if BOP changes sometimes lead to an apparently manipulated outcome.

I have a theory that a successful racing series should not only offer close and competitive racing, but should also feature cars that fans would eagerly watch even if only one was driving around alone. Such a car needs to be obviously 'on the edge', the driver's steering, brake and throttle inputs averting disaster by the narrowest of margins. I recall years ago at Oulton Park, watching Tiff Needell's recalcitrant Saab 900 approaching Old Hall corner. Despite this being a somewhat uninteresting race car, what was so memorable is that Tiff was still on the start-finish straight whilst pointing in the general direction of Cascades and fully on the steering lock stops! Such a display of sublime car control was utterly inspirational but only made possible by a difficult-to-drive race car.

INSIDE TRACK

A challenging track design is fundamental to the racing spectacle. It is a vital element that allows drivers the opportunity to differentiate themselves from the rest of the field, even taking into account the overwhelming influence of the race car as detailed in the 1am It's A Set-Up chapter. It's what excites us about places like the Nordschleife, the mountain at Bathurst, the Corkscrew at Laguna Seca and of course the infamous Eau Rouge-Raidillon sequence at Spa. Reducing or removing these challenges diminishes the essence of what motor racing has come to represent over its long history.

The indestructible driver mindset, added to the enormous pressure that especially younger competitors feel to compete even in apparently dangerous conditions, leads to elevated risks such as my own 'blind' driving in rain or fog described earlier in the 4am The Feeling chapter. It is abundantly clear that drivers in general will not back off or elect not to race in these circumstances. It is for the organisers and circuits to make sure driver (and spectator) safety is not compromised, even stopping a race if conditions are too dangerous. However, this does not have to mean dumbing down the track or the nature of the asphalt surface between the white lines. That route leads to obscurity as drivers and particularly spectators, the lifeblood of motorsport investors, become bored and look elsewhere for their entertainment.

My considered opinion of track design is that, first and foremost, it should require a great deal of skill to navigate competitively, even without the distraction of other cars ahead or behind. Some will cite construction space or cost as a reason for adopting somewhat mundane layouts, but these restrictions do not prevent for example the intelligent use of camber or small elevation changes, to increase the driving challenge.

Imagine a classic tightening right-hand corner after a high-speed section. Add a crest or two to the track surface midway through the braking zone and introduce a positive camber deepening into the apex of the corner to reward an earlier turn in. On the ideal line, that combination will destabilise the car as the driver attempts to brake with some steering lock applied. More fun and games can be had if the crests are built to be less severe on the left side. The driver is now faced with a compromise: take the ideal line braking over the crest straight towards the helpful apex camber, or brake later and straighter on the smoother left-hand side and run deeper into the corner, initially losing the benefit of the camber but increasing the overall radius of the corner perhaps for a faster exit.

Simple tweaks like these can be incorporated into circuit resurfacing, raising the level of driver competence required as well as increasing out-braking opportunities, even if the circuit map appears unchanged. At Castle Combe, the high-point for me was always Quarry corner, a real test of skill somewhat similar to the long right-hander illustration above, but originally with the added complexity of the braking zone featuring a blind left-hand kink over a crest. During practice, I lost control of our lightweight 'Sud there, braking late and trying to fight the car across to the left to gain the optimum turn in to the critical right-hand apex. In the name of safety, subsequent resurfacing of the track there actually reduced the severity of the crest and consequently lessened the challenge, as I discovered when I returned in 2005 to drive a Ginetta.

Dingle Dell at Brands Hatch is another sad loss, the original exhilarating leap over the hilltop (somewhat like Knockhill's fabulous chicane) having been flattened before the 2003 season and eventually replaced with a more traditional right-hander. I recall James Thompson's 12g shunt there in the BTCC Honda. Despite the uninformed talk at the time about the danger of this corner, a more concerning issue was not the track configuration but the banning of tyre-warmers in 2000, in an attempt to restrict costs towards the end of that wonderful Super Touring era.

Another such track rework occurred at Quiddelbacher Höhe at the Nordschleife, a much more significant crest, over which GT3 cars especially would famously pull a 'wheelie'. Imagine seeing little but sky for a brief moment, right before the 130mph (210kmh) blind double-apex right-hander at Flugplatz. The appalling 2015 crash there, when a Nissan GT3 vaulted the safety fence, distressingly killing a spectator and injuring others, resulted in a temporary 200kmh speed control approaching and through that section and a flattening of the preceding crest. The combination of this original track feature, the GT3 aerodynamic specification, and drivers' enthusiasm to maximise Flugplatz cornering speed due to the following flat-out section to Schwedenkreuz, led to the limit being exceeded with dire consequences.

Notwithstanding the emotions and sympathies of that terrible day, should the track have been modified? I think not and I am not alone. If spectator safety opposite the approach to the corner could not be guaranteed, even with further enhanced safety fencing, then making that a spectator-free area should have been sufficient. It should remain the duty of the drivers to respect the elevation changes of the track, difficult as that may be, as they must in every other section of the Green Hell.

Sections of other circuits, again including Eau Rouge–Raidillon at Spa, also feature somewhat extreme natural geography, partially limiting driver sight-lines. In fact, this particular corner sequence is often the site of accidents because it is unusually challenging relative to the rest of the track and should be approached with that appreciation. Here and in other such cases where vision is obscured, we rely heavily on the marshals' flag signals or trackside warning lights, but often these cannot be deployed quickly enough, as I once found when I emerged from the flat-out sixth-gear Fuchsrohre, to suddenly be confronted with almost stationary traffic, being unsighted through the quick blind left up into the second-gear Adenauer–Forst switchback.

Sometimes the implications of these blind sections are far more serious, with injuries or even fatalities leading to panicked calls for the circuit to be altered in that location. The answer is not to bulldoze the hill at Raidillon, nor to build up Eau Rouge with its red earth. When a climber falls off a cliff-face, authorities don't rush in to bolt a ladder to the mountainside in that location. The answer is to continually improve safety countermeasures without removing the challenge.

In the case of motor racing, through its links to the automotive industry, we have sophisticated and ever-more intelligent computing technology for example, which could be deployed as an instant warning system both trackside and on-board the race cars. Road car development of V2V (vehicle-to-vehicle) communication systems is well-advanced, allowing cars to wirelessly transmit their speed, position and direction to others around them; this system should be developed for mandatory use on the race track, instantly illuminating a steering wheel warning light or giving an audible warning of a hazard on track. Maybe in low visibility, even a progressive cut in power would be helpful when a spun or crashed car is detected ahead. The challenge of the track can then be maintained, along with the quality of the racing spectacle.

There is also an historical element that we have a duty to preserve, especially with 'classic' tracks. These have so much more character than artificial modern constructs painted onto featureless former carparks, that remove all reference to the past geography of the landscape beneath. I see this as part of an image problem for Formula E, when it chooses to create very contrived corners in obviously-temporary and characterless city street circuits such as the London ExCeL track, an unconvincing venue marked out with concrete or plastic barriers like a glorified go-kart track. Their Monaco event is so much more appealing.

One of the great attractions of motorsport for me is the relationship the car and driver forms with the history and the underlying landscape around the track. I love the fact that it is still possible to recognise how our most enduring venues were often constructed from a combination of ancient roads (like the Nordschleife), manorial estate driveways (like Oulton Park) or aircraft runways (like Silverstone), connected to form a circuit for racing.

Back in 2016, after I'd shunted the Aston in an unrecoverable location, the race ended and as the marshals were obliged to leave the track within the hour, I was left standing totally alone between Kesselchen and Klostertal in the late afternoon sunshine by the trackside. There were even no spectators there, only the steep forested hillsides resonating with birdsong. At that peaceful and reflective moment, I found it fascinating to imagine that long ago, maybe a tree fell, forcing wildlife to divert around it, forming a winding forest path which over the following centuries was used by human hunters and later farmers and miners even as they cleared away the trees. Over the years the path became wider and more deeply inscribed by horse and cart, but still following that time-worn route curving around the site of the fallen tree. Perhaps as I waited for the team to appear that day, I was looking at that same sequence of curves, now framed with Armco barriers and painted kerbing, earth and roots obscured with asphalt. The valley reverberating with the roar of racing engines and the shriek of a locked-up slick would have been utterly alien in that ancient woodland where the tree fell.

I should add at this point there are other magnificent and often little-known tracks available which make excellent use of their natural geography, all being worthy of a visit by any driving enthusiast. For example, Circuit du Mas du Clos (between Limoges and Clermont-Ferrand), reopened in 2022, has never been sanctioned for racing but features challenging mid-corner camber changes, blind crests and plenty of high-speed sections. Alternatively, try the Ring Knutstorp, a half hour east of Helsingborg, a short undulating circuit with a fantastic concentration of cambers, crests and compressions, especially in the second half of the lap. To me, it seems like a smaller-scale version of the Autódromo Internacional do Algarve at Portimão, a much more familiar circuit since playing host to Formula 1 through the COVID-19 years.

A side effect of such interesting topography, especially if the corners in question are critical to lap time, is that it may necessitate set-up changes to the cars, to mitigate any negative response of the car to the terrain. Such changes will mean the set-up is probably not ideal elsewhere around the track, placing more demands upon the driver and as a side effect, improving the racing spectacle. In this respect, we've already looked at the steeply-banked concrete of the Karussell on the Nordschleife and the ride height compromise it necessitates. Some record-setting cars like the Porsche 919 Hybrid Evo in 2019 even elect to drive around the top of the Karussell to avoid the problem, considering that the time lost in that section is worth the benefit elsewhere around the lap. Sadly, in a racing environment, that line will likely result in lost track position, tyre pick-up from all the 'marbles' off-line, or in the worst case a puncture from all the shards of carbon-fibre up there. Consequently, we must dive into the Karussell and therefore cannot run the cars as low as we would like, heightening the demands upon the drivers.

The keyword here is compromise. A consistent track surface with a single optimal racing line requires no compromise and leads to trains of cars and dull races, necessitating artificial manipulation by introduction of DRS for example. A well-designed track should offer options for multiple approaches, none being perfect, forcing drivers to consider different lines and set-up options. The optimal solution will also be influenced by factors such as tyre wear, fuel load, brake temperatures and track conditions, the goal being to maximise the available surface around every lap. Up to this point, we have only considered the available surface to be the 'black stuff' between the white lines bordering the asphalt. In my view, precisely the same consideration should be given to the surface immediately beyond those white lines, presenting drivers with further options to find lap time.

Increasingly this is becoming a point of contention, with apparently contrived 'track limits' dominating the commentary. In June 2023 for example, more than 30 track limits penalties were handed out during qualifying for the Thruxton BTCC event. Even more puzzling for spectators, during the session, a tyre stack marking the Club chicane was knocked out of place but five minutes or so went by with cars straight-lining the chicane before the red flag was shown: their lap times were still counted because there was no track limits observer stationed at that corner! Oddly, the Motorsport UK judgement of what constituted a breach of track limits was different to the FIA rule of 'at least one wheel on the white line' employed at the Austrian Grand Prix the following month. There, over 40 track limits penalties were observed in the Formula 1 qualifying session, followed by several during the race and, shamefully, eight more hours after the chequered flag, which significantly adjusted the final classification. Some of the best drivers in the world were even complaining that they could not tell if they were over the white line or not! Perhaps an audible rumble strip would be a solution. Nevertheless, it's no surprise that fans of the sport were confused and disaffected, preferring to watch alternative forms of racing where the chequered flag, not the stewards' office, actually determines the finishing order.

I strongly believe track limits should simply be determined by how far a driver can go without losing time. It's up to circuit designers to introduce features to control that limit by slowing the cars that excessively exploit it. Nobody intentionally exceeds track limits at the Nordschleife, because if they do, they'll certainly lose time, likely damage the car, or worse, experience a race-ending crash. On a more traditional circuit suited to single seaters, the enormous run-off areas and low kerbs mean alternative methods are required to dissuade drivers from abusing the intended track limit. An obvious solution is a corner entry or exit kerb which should never be wider than a car's width if the intent of the circuit designer is for the cars to keep at least one wheel on the white line. Beyond that there should be a disadvantageous feature, be it heavily-serrated concrete, grass or gravel as seen at the exit of Silverstone's Luffield, for example. We probably don't need to go as far as the creative suggestion of my daughter Amelie: sensor-triggered sheets of fire!

In any case, circuit designers need to accommodate all forms of racing, including motorcycles, sometimes limiting their choice of track limit control solutions. Some options are clearly ill-considered: recent experiences with temporary raised 'sausage' kerbs for example, launching Alex Peroni's F3 car into the catch fencing at Monza's since-renamed Parabolica or injuring Abbie Eaton's spine at COTA, show that this is a clumsy device, which can bring unintended and horrific consequences. More innovative solutions such as adjustable-height kerb elements for specific events should not be out of the question. Alternatively, we can ask my local council to resurface the borders of the track: terrifying potholes will appear there in no time!

More seriously, I am quite sure, having had a lot to do with the chemical industry over my professional life, that it is possible to engineer low-friction coatings applied to a strip of asphalt just beyond the kerb, replicating the low level of grip we experience in the rain. You never see drivers intentionally exceeding track limits when the kerbs are wet: let's make it that way in the dry!

Furthering the theme of low grip, having already observed the much higher quality of racing in wet conditions, I've joked before that some corners of the track should feature water sprinklers to mix things up a little! Years ago, I attended an indoor kart track for a fun event and they had polished the concrete of one corner sequence, known as the Icy Curve. That corner made all the difference to an otherwise rather typical hairpin-infested circuit and I found myself looking forward to it every lap! Regardless of how it is achieved, drivers need to be tested to the limit by inventive track features and non-obvious surface conditions if we are to discern who is truly the most deserving winner.

ONE HELL OF A LAP

Now that you have my opinions about desirable race car attributes and ideal track designs, I'd like to share a driver's-eye perspective of a 24 hour race lap in one such car, at the most challenging circuit in the world: the Green Hell! More than that, if I have succeeded, it should take you approximately the same time to read as it takes to complete the lap in reality. Don't worry if it takes you a little longer: it was probably raining more heavily!

Before we embark on our lap, let's first talk about why I've chosen to share the experience at this circuit in particular. Racing legend and hero Sir Jackie Stewart originally gave the Nürburgring Nordschleife its famous nickname, the 'Green Hell' after his victory in the rainstorm and thick fog of the 1968 Grand Prix. It was an absolute privilege for me to meet Sir Jackie recently and talk about this book. Since 1970, the Green Hell has hosted the Nürburgring 24 hours endurance race in the forested Eifel mountains of northwestern Germany, attracting drivers and teams from all over the world, keen to prove their abilities in the toughest of conditions.

The race is contested on the original Nordschleife (first constructed in 1927) and the modern-day Formula 1 Grand Prix circuit (completed in 1984). As we've seen, the combination of these two tracks provides a unique set of conditions for the racing driver. With a single lap comprising almost 16 miles (over 25km), the huge variety of corners and gradients leaves very little time to relax. High levels of concentration and accuracy are required over long periods of time: typically, each driver is behind the wheel for two-hour stints in the 24 hour race. To put this into perspective, this is the same duration as a typical Formula 1 race, but the endurance racing driver must complete four such stints in 24 hours! On the Nordschleife there is also little scope for error: many corners and crests are blind, the kerbs are extremely aggressive and the barriers are very close to the trackside, meaning mistakes are often punished by a heavily damaged car.

In the past, more than 200 cars in a variety of classes took the start of the Nürburgring 24 hours race. More recently, with the slowest classes no longer permitted, the number is around two-thirds of that, but still with a lap time difference of more than two minutes between the fastest and slowest cars. This brings the risk of encountering slower competitors in a difficult spot, or conversely the risk of a faster car coming past at a great speed differential.

The Eifel is renowned for unpredictable weather conditions, with fog, rain, hail or even snow always a possibility. The length of the track means that part of the circuit can be dry whilst other sections may be streaming with water. A driver who has started a lap on slick tyres and then encounters rain has no choice but to complete the many remaining kilometres on those unsuitable tyres before a pit-stop for a tyre change can be made. In that time, the track could dry and a tyre change may in fact be inappropriate, meaning race strategy is an ongoing live discussion between driver and pit wall.

Given these variable weather conditions, the rate of attrition can be high; crash debris, oil or other fluids on the track are also a common hazard. The dark hours of the night present a further test, and unlike some other night race venues, there are no floodlights illuminating the circuit beyond the pit straight. Despite highly-advanced headlight systems, the geography of the track makes visibility a major issue. It is not uncommon even for highly-experienced drivers to return to the pits after a night-time stint with eyes wide, such is the immense challenge of racing the Green Hell!

So, it's 2am. You're asleep in one of the Dorint Am Nürburgring trackside hotel rooms, after successfully completing a closely-fought 24 hours starting stint, followed by another barbeque-scent-filled thriller as the sun sank behind the forested peaks to the west. Undisturbed by the thump of rock music from the fan-crowded hill opposite or the repetitive crescendo of passing racing engines, you're jerked into wakefulness by the phone alarm! Check the timing sheets on the TV: car's running fine, still P2 in class, made up a few overall places, team mate's doing a great job in survival mode.

Quick shower, fresh Nomex under jacket and trousers, then out on the balcony to check temperatures and weather. City lights on the horizon beyond the darkness of the Green Hell look indistinct and there's a cold wind blowing from the northwest judging by the pit lane flags: going to be tough to maintain the tyre pressures on the out lap. Check the weather radar app: light rain moving slowly in over the next couple of hours. That's our car thundering past on the pit straight below!

2:30am: time to go. Take the shortcut out of the hotel past the Cockpit Bar, avoid the raucous throng fumbling for their passes, through the old paddock and tunnel, quick glance at the Nordschleife map of racing legends up there on the wall. Up the slope into the paddock past the Mundorf Tank pumps, a waft of chips from the snack bar. Sudden loudness of passing cars triggers a brief palpitation of excitement. Fans carrying old slicks and Bitburger bottles, racing folks walking purposefully or dejectedly, depending upon their fortunes so far. Take the stairs up the race control tower to the balcony at the back of the pit suites. No crowd up here, Ravenol big wheel illuminating all those race truck roofs.

Straight down to the pit garage for a chat with the lead engineer: anything to report? Code 60 in Hatzenbach: that could be a bad one. Team mate reports car is working well in the cool of the night. Six laps to go in her stint. Glance up at the GPS map: she's at Pflantzgarten. What are the gaps? Right behind P1 in class and around three minutes ahead of #87 in P3. It's going to be neck-and-neck for P2 after our pit stop. Mechanics dozing in their camping chairs. Out to the race truck to change into race suit and boots. Headphones on, 'acceleration' playlist starts calmly with a bit of Wolf Alice. Grab a banana, a cup of Tregothnan and the electrolyte drink bottle from the fridge. Find a quiet spot in the other truck to watch the screens and warm up with a resistance band. Playlist tempo peaks with some Pretty Vicious.

Check the GPS: she's at Döttinger Höhe, one more lap remaining. Hatzenbach Code 60's gone but double yellows in Fuchsrohre. Quick 'pit stop' stop in the garage before balaclava, HANS and helmet go on. Few more leg, shoulder and neck stretches, don't want cramps like a few years back. Mechanics all awake now, tools in hand, tyres wheeled in from the warming tent. Is that rain or just mist in the glare of floodlights? Boss on the pit wall has turned around, lead engineer out in the pit lane, car's coming in. Stand to the left side, seat insert in hand. Headlights approach, not ours, but she's right behind!

Car jerks to a halt, mechanics descend on wheels and fuel cap. Run around the back to the driver's door: already open, seat fully slid back and she's climbing out. Grabs her seat insert, yells something unintelligible, thumbs up. Seat insert in, one leg over the roll cage, the other squeezing in behind. Tang of hot metal, oil, brakes and fuel. Seat forward, engineer on the lap belts. Grab shoulder belts... wait! Make sure they're seated properly on the HANS. Drink and radio connected? Check. Safety net in place, door slams. "*Radio check, radio check...*" Driver ID, mirrors, fuel reset, ABS and TC settings... good to go. Windscreen guy on the bonnet jumps off, car clunks down on the jacks, fuel nozzle rattles out, engineer's finger circles, fire it up. First gear, lollipop up, boot it out of there with a squeal of rubber!

Dark sky against the lights of the pit lane... gearbox whines, telemetry screen bright on the dash, already counting fuel and stint times. Green light, pit lane speed limiter off, go, go, go! Slight curve right, don't cross the pit exit line, watch the left mirror, headlights in the distance, no trouble. Tighter entry than usual into Yokohama S, brake a bit earlier, watch the

249

bump on the apex. Quick squirt, chop left over the second apex than power out over the green concrete... still seems dry and grippy enough.

Third, fourth then brake by the NLS circuit cut-through and down to third again for the Valvoline Kurve. Use the positive camber, balance feels good... let it run out then fight it back over for the Ford Kurve. Brake deep into the apex then hard on the throttle through to the exit kerb, right up to the gravel. Fans still there waving flags in the grandstand... cool!

Power down the hill, check the mirror, headlights still there? Up to fifth then super-late trail braking, all the way down to second gear, rotate the car into the on-camber Dunlop Kehre hairpin. Patient on throttle, let it wash out over the exit kerb, quick mirror check and cross back over for the Schumacher S. It's never flat, a quick lift, brush that apex kerb up the hill... twitch over the bump, watch the gravel scattered over the right-hand kerb.

Headlights gaining in the mirrors, flashing blue light, probably a GT3. Brake just past the gantry for RTL Kurve and get the car right over the apex concrete. Always slippery here, use the exit kerb, pull it back left and brake deep into the Warsteiner Kurve. OK, he's almost with me... hang on, there are two of them...!

All over the exit kerb, stay left... they won't pass me before the Advan Bogen so take the shortest line, avoid the marbles. Burst of flame under the red balloon off to the left. Glance to right mirror, move across, up to fifth, Grello Porsche GT3 whips past under braking before 50m board into the NGK Schikane, wait for that second GT3... then turn in. It's an Audi, chucks gravel up on the flat right-hand apex. Usual touch of oversteer in third on exit, bring it across to mid-track, now brake deep and take second up into the left apex... and we are onto the Nordschleife!

Kill the slide as the camber flattens, skim the blue-and-red wall and snatch third over the crest. Over the old pit lane exit and down into second into the apex of Sabine-Schmitz-Kurve. Early throttle, tickle the kerb to get that exit nailed. Fourth down the hill, just a small lift, no brake into Hatzenbach Bogen... graze the narrow concrete strip on the exit, watch the bumps here in Hatzenbach.

What's that acrid smell, something burning? Yellow-and-red board showing on right, likely mud on track from apex cutting, hold it left then cut right to straighten it over the dirt. Watch the plastic barrier on the left, lot of debris there! Hard on the gas in third out of here, smooth through the next cambered left, quick brake, don't take the high kerb on the right (it's not qualifying!), pitch it left, nudge the tight exit kerb, across to the left and feel the front into the falling blind right at Hocheichen. Can't see the exit over the crest... there it is! Fully lit onto the rumble strip, quick brrrrr through the hands, blur of cameras at the exit fence and we're away.

Tyre pressures coming up nicely, headlights picking up the narrow bridge and tail-lights in the distance. Thread it between the concrete walls over the bump and there's the crest at Quiddelbacher Höhe... light brake, downshift and grab the first apex, trust it, it'll make the second, check the exit speed at the Flugplatz kerb. Crackle on the radio... Code 60 at Fuchsrohre..."Copy." Burning smell stronger now, displays look good, no sign of smoke in the cockpit.

Sixth-gear, banks of mist hanging low over the tarmac in the Kottenborn hollow... keep right where the jump's less severe. Check the mirrors, brake, snatch fifth, trust the speed over the bump through Schwedenkreuz. Let it drift out, now brake hard across to the left, gravel trap's right there, tip it into the long apex at Aremberg and get back on it early.

Flashing yellow light trackside... this'll be for that Code 60. Under the bridge through the bumpy wiggles down to Fuchsrohre, yellows on the right, keep off that line of fluid on the left, stand on the brake down to 120kmh... traffic ahead, purple Code 60 boards, hard brake and 60kmh speed limiter button. Marshals in orange, rescue truck, car on fire on the left under the trees in the compression at the bottom. Must've been that burning smell.

Crawling up behind a Cupra TCR... dammit he's only doing about 50kmh! Quick drink, green board up at the fast left, release the limiter, no need to use that wide apex kerb at this speed. Power around the outside of that Cupra... wait, has he seen me? Down to second for the sharp left at Adenauer-Forst, always slippery through here. Hold it tight, hold it tight, now flick it right, full throttle along the kerb and down to Metzgesfeld 1.

Cool fireworks over the track on the left! Mirror check, keep it flat through the first curve, tip-toe through the second up to the grass edge, ghostly faces in the trees at Metzgesfeld 2. Dark line on the track into left... take a wider apex. Back-end's moving over the right-hand crest, straight back onto brakes down into the camber at Kallenhard. Follow the apex around... now fire it out of here, just kissing the exit kerb and move over to nail the left-hand apex at Spiegelkurve... watch the understeer, tight here. Slow Toyota blocking into Miss-Hit-Miss... wait, wait, wait until he commits, now go to his left, watch the bump out here on the exit, right up against the Armco.

Big brake on the downhill before Wehrseifen, ease off for the right kink, hit it again for the hard left, down to second and connect with the apex. Careful on the throttle out of here. Keep it nailed through the gentle right...lots of fans still up there on the bank. Get it straight for braking into Breidscheid... there's a car ahead already turning in between the walls. Trust the front end, let it wash out, it'll pick up grip mid-corner. Quick brake dab into Ex-Mühle now back on it. Use the hill to rotate the car, watch the traction and stay off that grabby kerb!

Closing up on that other car, it's a BMW... too quick to get by before the Lauda Links (fleeting thought here for Niki). BMW's moving left, dive through on the right into Bergwerk. He's braking super-late, bumpy and dirty as hell on this side, need to keep the overlap inside and cut him off! Use the apex camber and punch the throttle early, long climb coming. Check the speed at the surface change, few kmh down thanks to the BMW. Flat out into left, left, left but stay on the line, gets dewy under the trees.

Hard left coming up at Kesselchen: don't think about the old shunt here and those nice Swiss marshals, keep the right foot on the floor! Is that the first blue light of dawn in the sky? Mirror check, all good... engine howling, sixth-gear just before Klostertal to look after it. Trust the car over the bumps, back down to fifth, exhale and carry the speed through the Mutkurve apex, just touching the exit concrete. Quick lift over the crest on the blind right... no name and no run-off! Get positioned then heavy on the brakes tight into the Steilstrecke... loads of fans up there. Smooth surface here: gas it around the long apex kerb, shudder of traction control over the bump on the exit.

More red tail-lights dropping out of sight up the hill ahead... just time for a quick flash to the British marshals on the left. Spot the braking into the Karussell just past the corner of the concrete apron. Thump, thump, thump, thump around the banking, stay off the black stuff... let it wash out over the end and easy on the throttle for the drive shafts. There are those tail-lights again.

Slight confidence-lift up through the fast left and... Hold on! Track looks damp! Wary on the brakes into the left, g-force in the seat washing out into the right at Höhe Acht. Like ice up over the top, car steps out on power, quick grabs of opposite lock, couple of bites to get it turned into the exit. Gently on power, open the steering over the crest towards Hedwigshöhe. What's that car ahead? Any spray from his tyres? Two clicks more ABS and ease the brakes on early into Wippermann... stay off the left and right kerbs, this car doesn't like them. Definitely damp but not wet.

Careful on the turn into the uphill right at Eschbach, understeer over the top not that bad. Track seems drier into the long downhill left. Square it off into Brünnchen, cut right over the drop off, run right out onto the grasscrete strip: brrrrrrrr, short brake, throw it in again and brrrr up to the raised kerb... good grip here. ABS to dry setting and get back on it! Lots of campfire smoke across the track, smells like a barbeque! Maybe the wind's changed? Trail-brake left up into the apex of the Eiskurve, keep off the big old exit kerb and fight it right before the twists down to Pflanzgarten... that's the #87 ahead!

Stick the brakes before and after the jump and throw it in on the camber. Wriggle of understeer over the crest left, get it straight and time the gear shift over the Pflantzgarten 2 jump. Not quite full throttle until a bit further through the Stefan Bellof S... watch that hidden apex kerb on the left, don't need the exit concrete. All over the #87 now! Jink right to Schwalbenschwanz... Whoa! White flag, slow Lambo there, rear tyre flailing, bits everywhere. Back across then fight it right to get the better run through the left-hander.

Straight shot to the Kleine Karussell, wide into the shallow banking, speed building and jump out again tight as possible: he's gone wider. Up the rise to Galgenkopf and into fourth gear... mind that nasty bump after the first apex, half a lift, now hard back on the throttle down into the last right. Perfect, couple of car lengths off his bumper for the slipstream down the Döttinger Höhe! Couple more tail-lights in the distance... speed's creeping up in his draft, 251, 252, heard his gearshift just after mine. Are those more spots of rain on the windscreen? Quick radio check... well? "Still dry in the pit lane..." Good.

Switch right as he moves left up the rise, we've got the overlap now. Lots of wind noise, keep it pinned through Antoniusbuche... scheisse, he's running us right out to the dust! 275 down the hill into Tiergarten... exhale... don't lift before the compression. Get it straight over the crest, late on the brakes and all the way down to second for the Hohenrain chicane. We're past him! Use all that track on the left, chuck it through slow right, now blast out of here in third, shaving the exit Armco: those marshals could have touched the car!

Lights in the right-hand mirror, #87's dived into the pits, must've been running on fumes. Dip the headlights down the pit straight, re-tighten the shoulder straps, quick drink squirt, check the pit wall for a board and prepare for seven or eight more laps!

... and breathe...!

Driving the Green Hell in this twice-around-the-clock race tests every sense. Every stint is an intense, thrilling, utterly fulfilling experience and every lap brings the unexpected. For me, a dawn stint like this one is the most perfect, yet surreal, experience. After hours staring down the tunnel of headlights, the skies brighten slowly from blue to indigo to a faint pink, track visibility lengthens as the darkness retreats, the deep greens of the forest emerge, the mists clear and suddenly, a shaft of sunlight hits your mirrors on the Döttinger Höhe.

You and your team have survived the night; only ten more hours to the chequered flag!

THE FINISH LINE!

The chequered flag triggers a range of emotions according to circumstance, but in general it is relief, satisfaction and jubilation that occupy the podium. In particular, the completion of an endurance race yields extreme, teary reactions even from the most hardened individuals after the triumphant champagne spray has evaporated, giving way to a pause for quiet reflection.

Some say the elation of winning, vanquishing our opponents and proving our status as the best of the best, are the most prevalent and addictive qualities of motor racing. Now you've reached this finish line, I've hopefully conveyed it is the also the thrill of the driving experience itself and the close-quarter skirmishes with other competitors that repeatedly summon us back to the grid. If that is not motivation enough, the race driving career will be short-lived. Winning is simply a means to continue racing, to access more challenging and enjoyable cars and tracks and to convince sponsors and teams to foot the increasing bill.

Like any addiction, the racing buzz becomes normalised over time and requires ever greater stimulation to achieve the same high. This is undoubtedly the neural pathway evolution in my brain's limbic system that led me to the Green Hell, the greatest of all race track challenges. This magnificent circuit in its various guises has hosted grand prix or endurance racing for almost a century. On a track now deemed too unsafe for Formula 1, the Nürburgring 24 hours race and the NLS championship have survived for more than half that time. Both have a proud tradition of multi-class endurance racing, a key ingredient to allow aspiring racers gain experience (and nowadays the required Nordschleife race permit). This format also offers a stunning spectacle for hundreds of thousands of highly-enthusiastic fans, each race car passing or being passed more times in one 24 hour race than there are pages in this book.

Perhaps reading Racing Hell has given you pause to consider your preferred type of racing. Perhaps it will help advocate for truly authentic racing at all levels and venues. I would only caution that in an increasingly micro-managed zero-risk world, we may find such adrenalin outlets are eventually stifled and shut down. Will the Nürburgring 24 hours race remain unchanged in the face of 'progress'? It will not be enough to simply hope so.

We need to fight to preserve its heritage, its challenge and the opportunity it offers to those with sufficient ambition and talent to prove themselves in battle with the serpentine beast which lurks within the forested peaks and valleys of the Green Hell.

PADDOCK TALK

ABS	Anti-lock Braking System
Aero (dynamics)	The effect of airflow over the car's surfaces
Apex	Inner corner point intersected by the racing line
Aquaplaning	Loss of tyre contact with the road due to water
BOP	Balance of Performance equality adjustment
BTCC	British Touring Car Championship
Camber, off/adverse	Track sloping away from the corner apex
Camber, on/positive	Track sloping towards the corner apex
Camber (suspension)	Angle between the wheel and the vertical
Caster (suspension)	Top to bottom angle of the steering axis
Castrol R	An engine oil favoured by class car racers
Centre of gravity	The point of all combined masses in the car
Cherry Bomb	Noisy exhaust system with a minimal silencer
Chicane	A sharp left and right bend combination
Code 60	Temporary 60kmh limit in endurance racing
Contact patch	The area of the tyre touching the road surface
Corner	Track deviation needing major steering input
Corner weights	The static mass carried by each wheel
COTA	Circuit Of The Americas (near Austin, Texas)
Dampers	Shock absorbers, part of the suspension
Damper, bump	Resistance to damper compression
Damper, rebound	Resistance to damper extension
Differential	System transmitting power to driven wheels

Diffuser	Aero device to generate rear downforce
DNF	Did Not Finish
DNS	Did Not Start
DRS	Drag (Difficulty!) Reduction System
Double-header	Two races at the same event
Doughnuts	Tyre-sliding stunt leaving circular skid marks
Dow Automotive	A division of The Dow Chemical Company
Downforce	Vertical load of aero devices (opposite of lift)
ECU	Engine Control Unit
EERC	European Endurance Racing Championship
ERS	Energy Recovery System
FIA	Federation Internationale de l'Automobile
Fire off	Pushing another car off the track
Formula E	Single seater championship for electric cars
Four-wheel drift	Controlled slide of all wheels through a corner
Gravel trap	Area in corners to catch crashing race cars
Green Hell	Nickname for the Nürburgring Nordschleife
Grid	Track markings to position cars in start order
Grip, lateral	Ability of a tyre to resist sliding sideways
GT (racing cars)	'Grand Tourer' long-distance high-speed cars
Hairpin	A typically 180° corner between two straights
HANS	Mandatory Head And Neck Support device
HSCC	Historic Sports Car Club
In lap	A lap culminating in a return to the pit lane
Italian Intermarque	BRSCC 80s-90s championship for Italian cars
Limit	A notional maximum speed at any track section
LMP	Le Mans Prototype
Load transfer	Dynamic movement of mass to each tyre
Lock-up (brakes)	Under-rotation of the wheel causing a skid
Map (engine)	Software controlling engine outputs

Mindfulness	Meditation method focused upon the present
NASCAR	National Association for Stock Car Auto Racing
Nitrous injection	Provides extra air and oxygen to the engine
NLS	Nürburgring Langstrecken Serie, formerly VLN
One-make racing	A championship of identical specification cars
Out lap	A preparation lap after exiting the pit lane
Opposite lock	Steering opposite to the direction of the turn
Oversteer	Rear end grip loss, car over-rotates
Paddock	Area for team race trucks and hospitality units
Parc fermé	Secure area where officials check the race cars
Pit (lane, garage)	Car maintenance area adjacent to the track
Pit (wall)	Trackside race location for lead engineers
Pitch	Car mass rotation about the transverse axis
Podium	Top three finishers' presentation platform
Pole position	Starting position of the fastest car in qualifying
Pro Am	Professional and Amateur drivers
Qualifying	Timed laps to determine the starting order
Racing Hell	Truly authentic, unadulterated motorsport
Racing line	The optimal (fastest) route around a race track
Rake	Car forward inclination angle to the ground
Ride height	Vehicle underbody height above the ground
Roll	Car mass rotation about the longitudinal axis
Roll centre	Point of force transfer from suspension to body
Rotate (the car)	To turn the car into the corner
Safety car	Car deployed to slow racers in a hazard period
Scandinavian flick	A rear slide rallying technique for sharp corners
Scrutineer	Official who checks race cars meet regulations
Set-up	Adjustment of car suspension, aero and engine
Shunt	Crash
Silver Arrows	Mercedes Grand Prix racing cars

Sim. racing	On-line racing using a race car simulator
Slick (tyres)	Racing tyres without grooves (unlike wet tyres)
Slip angle	Delta between tyre direction vs. travel direction
Slipstreaming	Following closely for aerodynamic advantage
Splitter	Aerodynamic device at the lower front of the car
Stig	Mysterious driver from the TV series 'Top Gear'
Targa Florio	Italian endurance road race, founded in 1906
Telemetry (data)	On-board computer tracking of car performance
TOCA	Organiser of the BTCC
Toe (suspension)	Angle between wheel and car longitudinal axis
Traction control	Applies brake to each wheel to preserve traction
Trail braking	Apply brakes whilst turning into the corner
Turning-in point	Corner entry point on the racing line
Understeer	Front end grip loss, car does not rotate enough
Unsprung weight	Car's weight not supported by the suspension
VLN	See NLS
WEC	FIA World Endurance Championship
Weight transfer	Motion of a car's weight around its roll centre
Wind tunnel	Device to measure aerodynamic performance

Made in the USA
Coppell, TX
30 November 2023

25032188R00163